SHAKE RATTLE AND ROLL

SHAKE RATTLE AND ROLL

Brian O'Donnell

Copyright © 2017 Brian O'Donnell

The moral right of the author has been asserted.

All rights reserved.

No part of this publication may be reproduced, stored in a retrieval system, or transmitted, in any form or by any means, without the prior permission in writing of the publisher, nor be otherwise circulated in any form of binding or cover other than that in which it is published and without a similar condition including this condition being imposed on the subsequent purchaser.

These stories are raw, unabridged and unaltered to ensure a typical yarn is expressed.

National Library of Australia Cataloguing-in-Publication entry

Creator: O'Donnell, Brian, author.

Title: Shake, rattle and roll / Brian O'Donnell.

ISBN: 9780648014607 (paperback)

9780648014614 (ebook)

Subjects: O'Donnell, Brian--Biography. Tractor driving--England--Biography. Farm life--England--Biography.

Cover and Typeset: Pickawoowoo Publishing Group

The author can be contacted on: bsodonsm@tpg.com.au

Table of Contents

Preface vii

Chapter 1: MYSTERY AND INTRIGUE 1

Chapter 2: THE PICKERING RALLY 33

Chapter 3: OVER THE MOUNTAINS 61

Chapter 4: HEADING NORTH BY NORTHWEST .. 119

Chapter 5: A NEW BEGINNING 149

Chapter 6: CHESTER-LE- STREET RALLY 171

Postscript: CHANTELLE 191

Preface

I spent many very happy weekends and some weekdays messing about with Pride of the Road. I could not help but make comment on the magnificent scenery that we passed through. There is non better anywhere in the British Isles [matter of opinion] however I did not set out to write about the historic buildings and natural scenery of North Yorkshire and only touched on them in passing. My book is about the wonderful people of the North of England who helped us on our way. They fed us and bedded us and showed us so much love and care. I often wonder if the affection was for Pride of the Road rather than her crew. My special thanks go to all those wonderful people who assisted us on our way. My special thanks also to my wife Sandra for her undying support and tolerance. I must make mention of my youngest son David. Without

David's help and computer skills all this would still be in my head and never see the light of day. The fun and camaraderie between all the other engine men and women was unreal even when we were rivals for the honours bestowed upon us. My Granddaughter Chantelle also made all this possible she is always ready to edit and comment. I also need to express my undying devotion to the wonderful team at Pickawoowoo publishing. Their patience and devotion were needed to get this book to publication, thank you Pickawoowoo.

Chapter 1

MYSTERY AND INTRIGUE

I jumped off the bus on my way home from school and crossed the miniscule village green in front of the Royal Oak pub. I had to pass near the old blacksmith's shop as I entered the driveway into our farmyard and garden. The blacksmith shop was being used again these days after many years of neglect and disuse. The junk had been cleaned out and the new occupant had moved in.

The new tenant wasn't a blacksmith as you might expect but was in fact our local village plumber called James Alderton who I was very friendly with. I often helped him with his plumbing work at weekends and during the school holidays, which provided me with a bit of pocket money and we worked well together.

James had always been a bit of a wild man and

he was no better now; maybe even worse than ever. We never knew what he was likely to do or say next. Despite his wild ways however, he was a very good tradesman and could be relied upon to do a good job when he finally got around to it. He was extremely unreliable time wise and was apt to dive off at a tangent and race into something new at the drop of a hat, even when he was in the middle of an important plumbing job, leaving the poor client in dire straights until he got things sorted out and went back to finish up the job. James had fallen out with his first wife, which wasn't really surprising knowing James as we did, and when she left he had employed a housekeeper to look after his two children, a boy and a girl called Michael and Pauline, and keep house for him. He ended up marrying her when his divorce finally came through.

Pat was nearly as wild as James and they had many dingdongs along the way. Although Pat was a city girl she had more or less managed to fit in with James wild ways. She had learned to join in with village life and the plumbing business along with the daily hassle of housekeeping and looking after the kids. She was kept busy with a house to run and two school age children plus one recent arrival of her own, not to mention answering the telephone to explain her husband's possible whereabouts to concerned customers and other business related matters.

When in the late nineteen fifties some girls and women decided to go around topless in spite of our Yorkshire climate, Pat decided to give it a go. James escorted her on occasions to some of our local drinking houses including one very prestigious hotel alongside the A1 highway. Before entering the bar James picked up a very large stillson pipe wrench which he swung by his side as a warning to any of the young fellows who fancied their chances.

Today as I was passing the old forge James stuck his head out of the side door and called out to me, "Now then young man, school over for another week is it then?'

'Aye, it is that Mr Alderton." I replied. "Except for a fair bit of 'omework that is.'

'Aye well then that's grand Brian. 'Ave you got anything on in t'morning then?'

He asked me.

'Yea well, that's a good point Mr Alderton. You

see I won't really know until me Dad gets 'ome a bit later on. He might need a bit of a 'and with summat and I won't know for sure 'till I get to talk to 'im, and that might be latish on tonight. 'Why are you asking? Do you need a hand with one of your plumbing jobs then?' I asked him.

'Yea well, I've gotten plenty of work on, I allus 've as you know, but I've decided to take t'morning off you see. I've decided to drive over to Daltonby. I thought you might like to come for a ride with me and keep me company. You'll find it very interesting, I'm sure, if you can get away.'

'Right you are then Mr Alderton. As soon as me Dad gets 'ome I'll ask him about it and come right over to let you know what's 'appening if that's ok with you.' I answered.

'Aye, right you are then, that'll 'ave to do for now but you won't forget, will you?' James replied.

'No of course not. I'll be round as soon as I know what Dad's up to. What's on at Daltonby that's so important then?' I enquired.

'Aye well I'll keep that under me 'at until we get there but you won't be disappointed I'm sure.' Said James as he disappeared back into the smithy.

When Dad finally arrived home from work

I approached him about the trip to Daltonby. Dad said, in reply to my question about the next mornings work schedule.

'Oh aye what's he on with now? Will it be summat to do with his work or is it some hair brained bloody scheme that 'es up to again? Now look 'ere you'll 'ave to get all your chores done properly 'affore you go. I don't want to come home tomorrow night and find you've skived off and left half of your jobs for me to do. I suppose this is another of his crazy get rich schemes. Didn't he tell you what its about?'

'No he said it was a bit of a secret like.' I replied. "I got stuck into it my jobs straight away when I got home from school and I only need to feed the pigs and poultry in the morning. I've already done most of the other jobs.'

'Aye well you'd better be right about that otherwise there'll be 'ell to pay when I get 'ome tomorrow night. 'Ave you gotten all your 'omework done as well then?'

'Oh aye it's all done and the pigs have been cleaned out and new bedding put in their boxes.'

'Right you are then. Off you go and try to keep out of trouble. You know what a mad bugger

James can be.' These were Dad's final words on the matter.

I ran across the road to let James know that I would go with him provided that it wasn't to be too early. I told James, 'My Dad doesn't need me tomorrow so I can go with you to Daltonby but I have some chores to do before I can go if that's ok with you. I've pigs to feed and t'old 'ens to see to first'

'Yea well, that'll suit me 'cause I got a couple of jobs to finish up first so I'll call for you when I'm ready if that's ok?' James stated.

'Yea I'll be ready for you. What's on in Daltonby anyway?'

'It's a bit of a secret see, but you'll be surprised and you'll love it. It's right up your alley. You'll see. We're going to look at a bit of machinery, a bit of history really.'

'Ok then, I'll get up early so I'll be ready when you are, Mr Alderton.' I replied.

I was up early next morning, lit the fire and put the kettle on to boil whilst I fed the pigs and poultry before cooking up some breakfast. I had to get my chores done early in case I got held up but all went well. I fed and cleaned out the pigs first then let the poultry out to forage in the field behind the barn. Some of our hens were housed in the big barns (deep litter style) and needed to be fed and watered. It was too early yet but there were still quite a lot of eggs to collect, grade, and pack. I was finishing off a nice cup of tea when I heard James pull into our yard. I ran out and jumped into his old Austin van without any delay and away we went. I liked going around with James. He was so unpredictable and I could never tell what would happen next. James seemed to be unusually quiet this morning as we travelled along the main road towards the lovely village of Daltonby. All I managed to get out of him was a bit of a mention of looking at a tractor, which only deepened the mystery. The words James and tractors were hardly likely to be issued in the same breath in our normal daily lives so I was all 'agog' with anticipation. I sensed that today was going to something very special in my humdrum existence.

Daltonby was a very pretty little farming village about 12 miles away. In keeping with many other Yorkshire villages it had been built around a delightful babbling brook because of the need of it's residents to obtain a supply of household water before the days of modern 'piped in' water supplies.

The main street meandered alongside the stream or beck as they are called in this part of Yorkshire. There was a humped back bridge at either end constructed of sandstone to give access to the delightful row of thatched roof, stone cottages on the other side. The proud owners of the quaint cottages sported beautiful gardens with riotous displays of flowers such as geraniums and chrysanthemums and hollyhocks. There was a row of luxuriant weeping willow trees along the banks of the stream with their branches trailing down into the water. There were many ducks, coots and moorhens paddling around in the water or resting on the grassy areas nearby. The trees were alive with songbirds such as robins, wrens, finches, blackbirds, just to mention a few. They were darting around in the branches and scouring the grassed areas for the odd titbit, worm or grub. Daltonby was a must see village for any serious tourists but we had other agendas to attend to today.

As I well knew James was not one for scenery and pretty flowers. We were headed straight for the local pub known as 'The Jolly Farmer' which was a tourist highlight in it's own right because it was full of historic memorabilia but I knew that there would have to be a better reason than that for our visit, in spite of James's tendency to require large quantities of our local beers. The pub was also well known throughout the area for the high quality of it's nutty flavoured ales and beers, which in itself would have been a strong incentive for a visit from our intrepid plumber but it was still too early for that to be the reason for our trip. However, James pulled the old van up in front of the Jolly Farmer Pub. It was a pretty little village inn, which was typical of the area with whitewashed walls and flower boxes beneath the bay windows full of geraniums and other annuals providing a riot of colour. James jumped out of the driving seat and as he headed away from the van I called out after him. 'They won't be open yet, will they'?

'No, your right about that, it's still too early. Come on. Get off your arse, we've come to see the landlord. He's expecting us, see! We'll 'ave to go around to the back door though'.

When we entered the back yard we saw a very

large rotund gentleman standing on the neat little lawn feeding his ancient old dog. It was a very old black Labrador who stopped eating only long enough to give us a quick watery eyed inspection. Having satisfied himself that we were no threat to his master or himself he settled back to the task of finishing his breakfast.

'Aha! There you are' the landlord called out to us. 'You found the place a'wright then. You must be James Alderton but who's this young man here with you? 'Is 'e one of your lads then, James?"

'Aye I'm James and this is my neighbour's lad Brian. I reckon he might make a handy fireman one day if he shapes 'is self up a bit.' James replied with a wicked little chuckle.

'Right you are then we'll get cracking. We've just about finished 'ere like. Can we fit old Rex 'ere into your van. He enjoys a ride now and again and he likes a change of scenery. He doesn't get out of t'yard much these days. He's like me really, 'is old legs will 'ardly carry him around anymore'.

'Oh aye, he can sit in t'back in among the tools with Brian if we can lift him up.' James answered.

Once we got Old Harold settled in the front and Rex in the back Harold said, "Right we are then let's get cracking or else it'll be opening time afore we get there and back. Just drive straight down the village past yon post office. She's in an old farm yard right on the edge of t'village. The gate is just passed that old barn on the left hand side."

James stopped near the gate and I hopped out to open it. We entered a little- used farm enclosure behind the barn and there it was hidden beneath a heavy-duty tarpaulin. We pulled up besides a massive piece of machinery with a tall chimney sticking out at one end and what appeared to be a large flywheel holding up the tarp in the middle. The rear wheels were about 6 or 7 feet in diameter and the front ones about 4 feet diameter. After I had helped Rex out of the van I started to say, 'What the heck is ---?"

When James shouted out, 'Come on then Brian stir yourself. Let's get this tarpaulin off and "ave a good look at her. We 'aven't got all day you know and Harold 'as a pub to run.'

When the tarpaulin was pulled away James said, 'By heck you've really looked after the old lady Harold. Look at all that grease on t'gears and t'motion. It looks like all we need to do is fill up t'boiler and light a fire in t'firebox and we're away'

'Aye, you're right there James most contractors just walked away from these old steam engines and left them to rot when they replaced them with a tractor. Some of them were just hauled away for scrap metal but this one was like new and in fine fettle. I always looked after the old girl 'cause she was my living. She weighs 10 ton and I've been pestered many a time to sell her for scrap over the years but I alus wanted to see her steam away from 'ere one day. I always feared that t'scrap men would sneak in here and steal all the brass fittings if they got a chance. She was built at Marshalls of Gainsborough in 1910 and she's rated at 8 horse power.' Harold told us proudly.

'What made you hang on to this one then. You were never likely to use her again were you?' James asked.

'Well to tell you the truth James I must 'ave been a bit soft in t'head I think. You see when I started threshing corn I only had an old Fowler engine and when the fire box needed a major repair and the motion overhauled I decided to order a new engine direct from the Marshall works and this one is very special. I 'ad a bit of brass (money) around at that time and I wanted her to look really good so I got them to put extra brass fittings on her. The brass belly-bands are twice the size of normal ones and that big brass top on the chimney was extra as well. By heck I tell you she looked right bonny in that lovely maroon coloured livery. She was the best looking engine for miles around 'ere I can tell you. I was that proud of her you see. I couldn't bear the thought of her ending her days on some scrap heap. All chopped up with the oxy/acetylene torch. You know James I've walked down here with my dog every few weeks and turned the flywheel over to keep it free and then I checked her over for rust as well. You're right an all you know, all you 'ave to do is fill her up and light the fire. By heck I can't wait to see you drive her through t'village again. Just make sure you give me a good long blast on the whistle as you go past my pub.'

'Right you are then we'll take her as we agreed and we'll collect her next Saturday morning, so long as my fireman 'ere can get a day off. I tell you what, we might even stop in at the Jolly Farmer pub down the road for a pint 'affore we set off home.'

I piped up, 'You can bet your life on it Mr Alderton. I'll get all me jobs done early an I'll be ready and waiting for you. Has the engine got a name like most of the other steam tractors Mr. Harold?'

'Oh aye she does that, she's called "Pride Of The Road" and she was that I can tell you. T'names on a brass plate on the front of the smoke box door, and there's another nameplate in t'bar of my pub that you can 'ave as well. It was screwed onto the side of the foot rail and I was frightened that somebody might pinch it so I kept it at the pub for safety.'

'Right you are then it's about time you got that pub open Harold. We'd better get cracking. We'll bring the boiler testing kit with us next week just to be sure it's safe but by the look of it we'll 'ave no worries on that score.' James said.

'You're right about that James. You see the old girl didn't do a great deal of work before I bought a case tractor and retired her. The fire box and boiler will last you for many years because I always looked after 'em. There's a tap ower yonder on that wall corner so you only need a hosepipe to fill 'er up.'

We took Harold and Rex home and of course James suggested that he 'ad better test the beer to make sure it was still fit for drinking. It needed a couple of pints just to be certain but he finally decided that it was of excellent quality so we could set off home.

We were both very quiet for a while as we drove along the country road and approached the A1 highway until, finally I asked 'What the heck are you going to do with an old traction engine in Staveley, James?'

'Not in Staveley, Brian, Every summer we're going to take her to all the steam rallies in the district. The first one is always at Pickering in early spring, then there's all the agricultural shows to attend as well as other rallies and shows. I can't wait to see her on the show ground. She's such a bonny engine and when she's polished up she'll look grand.' He answered.

'Are we going to drive her around on those rough iron wheels or do you intend to get a lorry to travel her about?'

'Oh aye the old girl is fully licensed for road haulage and we'll look out for an old fashioned trailer to carry extra coal and tools etc. Anyway, I can't afford to pay for a low loader to get us around so we'll just have to drive it.' James replied.

'Hey James' I said. 'The other day I saw a

contractor moving some of his plant through Knaresborough and he was towing a van behind his tractor. Could we get Joe Hewson (our local blacksmith) to weld up a tow bar to pull the Austin behind us so that we would be able to get home and leave the tractor along the way sometimes. That way we would have all your tools with us as well as storage space for coal."

'By heck now your talking. I suppose it would be easy enough to find somewhere safe to park the tractor until the next weekend. That would save a lot of messing about and we could go further afield if we felt like it. I'll go and see old Joe next week.' James replied.

The following Friday evening was a mad rush to get as many of my weekend chores out of the way as I could. I collected all the eggs that I could find and Mam pitched in to help pack them into crates for transport to the egg board. Then it was a heavy session of homework and school assignments to clear the decks. On Saturday morning I was up and about very early and many of my chores were done before daylight since most of the sheds had electric lighting. I was finished and ready for off before James arrived to collect me then we were away again.

Once we arrived at the yard it was all go. First the boiler had to be filled up with fresh water and the steam pipes blanked off. We then had to pump up the boiler with more water to pressurise it and test for leaks and any weakness but all went well. The safety valve was stripped and cleaned and reset. At last the boiler was ready for action so I laid a fire in the box and coaxed it into life whilst James reassembled the steam pipes. It takes about 2hrs to bring a boiler up to working temperature without risking damaging any part of it. Whilst we were waiting we got stuck into the polishing mode. All the brass-work had to be cleaned and polished until it shone. Harold would never forgive us if we set off with a dirty engine. The tarpaulin had to be packed away and stowed in the van and bags of coal transferred to the engine bunker. This was all so exciting watching the engine come to life like a living being. Gosh! What a great adventure we had ahead of us. Once the pressure came up we had to check and adjust the safety valve relief pressure setting to protect the boiler from explosion. Then we went around all the working parts again for a final oiling up of the bearings and we were ready. We were amazed that Old Harold hadn't put up an appearance as yet. Maybe our departure was too emotional for him to bear. James opened the steam valve with the gears in neutral and pulled on the flywheel. Hurrah!!! The big flywheel started to move on it's own and soon the motion was sliding backwards and forward under steam pressure alone. We left the engine running whilst we did our final checks of the bearings. Amazingly there was no noise whatsoever, only the gentle hiss of steam from the cylinder drain cocks, which were open to blow out any condensed steam until the cylinder reached working temperature. James worked around the engine with a large spanner adjusting all the steam glands and joints to prevent the steam from leaking out whilst I did a bit of polishing. The water pump which is used to top up the boiler had to be checked over as did the steam injector system used also to feed water into the boiler whilst under full pressure before James could take the engine up to full speed until the flywheel spokes were just a blur. Once the engine had had a good run James shut off the steam and we checked every part of the motor to make sure it was as good as we could make it. So there we were, we were ready to set off at last but where the heck was Harold.

Finally all was ready and we climbed aboard. Harold or no Harold we had to get going. It was going to be a long slow drive home at only 4 miles per hour (the legal limit on iron wheels). James selected low gear and as he moved back and forth I swung the great iron steering wheel to manoeuvre the tractor out of the corner and onto the road. The tractor had only two gears high and low. Reverse was actioned by reversing the steam valves so the engine went in the opposite direction. Once on the road James drove the Austin van up to the rear and I connected the towing frame to the tow bar. The blacksmith had done a good job and it fitted nicely. With a few lively toots of the whistle we were off slowly down the road into the village. James stayed in low gear so that I could get the feel of the steering, which was no mean feat. It needed 18 full turns of that great big cast iron wheel to go from one lock to the other. Fortunately the Jolly Farmer was quite close and I was getting the hang of it by the time we pulled up in front of the pub with much tooting of the whistle. All the village kids had rushed out at the first toot and were a real hazard as they milled around us. James decided that he had a huge thirst on and needed some lubrication for his throat so, leaving the old girl sizzling and hissing we climbed down and headed towards the pub door. We had been so busy with the tractor that we failed to notice Harold's huge bulk propped up in the doorway almost totally blocking it. Harold had a huge grin from ear to ear and came out to congratulate us on our efforts.

'By heck you lads 'ave done a grand job on her. She looks magnificent.' He called out. 'Well done. She really is 'PRIDE OF THE ROAD' again

Pulling himself up to his full height and looking very stern James declared.

'Now look here landlord, enough of this frivolity. A jolly nice pint of your very best bitter for myself if you please and a large shandy for my engineer here, cause he's too young for a pint and we'd better be having a couple of your excellent pork pies apiece to see us on our way.'

'Coming up right away young man,' Harold replied as he continued to gaze at the tractor. 'By heck that's a grand sight, now I know the old girl will be safe from the scrap men.'

After a hearty meal washed down with fine ale it was time to go. Old Harold gave us both a mighty hug and wished us a good journey. He was fighting back a flood of tears, which were about to engulf him, and surely would once we were out of sight. It seemed that the whole population of the village and a few passers by were out to see us off. Everyone was waving and cheering as we set off with the whistle tooting to warn the onlookers. I said to James, 'We might have to look at painting the van with Marshall red paint to match the tractor. It looks really daggy and spoils the scene.'

'Aye I was thinking of summat similar meself and I think you're right Marshall Red would be the colour. We might 'ave to see if we can get some paint to suit.' James answered.

I steered the engine onto the road with the van following nicely behind and James kept up a melodious racket on the whistle as we headed for home. We stayed in low gear until we were out of the village and on the open road. By then I was seriously getting the hang of the steering so James stopped to change into high gear for the rest of the trip. The front axle was steered with two large chains loosely fastened to the axle and wrapped around a drum on the firebox. The whole assembly was pretty crude and I soon realised that due to the necessary slack in the chains, it was impossible to keep the front wheels straight. The front axle just pivoted back and forth to the extent of the slack in the chains so the old girl just wiggled and waggled from side to side and it was more or less out of my control. All I could do was point the chimney in the general direction of home and hope for the best.

The first few miles were on country roads with very little traffic and all went well for a while but I was constantly aware that the A1 Highway or the Great North Road as it was commonly known loomed up ahead of us. I managed to keep the tractor on the tarmac road until we had to enter the A1 and travel along it for 2 or three miles. It was amazing to observe the other road users as they interacted with our monstrosity. No one seemed to get too upset as they weaved and dodged around us. Most of the drivers were rapt with wonder and curiosity at this 10ton monster rumbling down the road. They gave us a great deal of room and respect, partly due to our size and look of indestructibility compared to their miniscule cars and partly out of curiosity. Those 6ft diameter wheels made of solid steel made sure of a safe passage for us but it was a relief to pull off the highway onto the quiet village roads again. We had just travelled through the historic coaching town of Boroughbridge and across the old medieval stone bridges over the rivers Swale and Ure. The streets were amazingly narrow and busy, needing great care on my part if we were not to come to grief on the way through. The tractor is not equipped with running brakes only a crude parking brake with wooden blocks clamping on to a large steel drum. The only way to stop in an emergency was to heave the reversing bar backwards to change the steam valve into reversing the engine rotation. We had to stop just off the highway where there was a small stream close to the road so that we could top up the water tank. We found out that we had a range of about 12 miles without water then we had to fit the long suction hose on to the steam pump so that we could suck up a stream of water from the beck. Whilst we were filling up the water tanks we worked around the engine with oilcans to top up the lubricators on all of the bearings. The lubrication system was very crude to say the least and every drop of oil that we pumped in to the bearings and other moving parts ended up liberally splashed all over the engine and all over ourselves. We were going to have to spend a fair amount of time in the bath once we got home. I had planned to spend an evening out with school friends at our local dancehall and it would need a liberal amount of soap and water to make me presentable for the occasion. Before we moved off again James also went around the steam glands and tightened the adjusting bolts to bed the packing onto the moving shafts.

It's very difficult to explain the feelings of a steam tractor to the uninitiated. They start out as cold, hard, inert, heaps of scrap metal that simply come to life as soon as the first match is inserted into the firebox. As the fire begins to take hold and flare up they steadily come alive just like a big grizzly bear awakening from winter hibernation. Once working steam pressure is achieved they react like a wild animal. The drivers can feel the heat pumping through the pipe work until they become a vibrant pulsating powerful machine ready for work. You can feel the inert power surging through it's veins as it stands by ready for off. They are responsive to every touch of the controls. Every noise, and there are plenty of those, tells a part of the story as they thunder down the road. Only a few of the moving parts are fitted with guards. The great metal wheels and cogs whirr around with wild abandon and woe-betide any body part that gets too close. Instant amputation is never far away and agonising pain can easily engulf the unwary operator or even onlookers. Added to all this is the steam leaking out of the various joints, boiling hot metal everywhere, the special smells of burning coal and hot oil which all add up together to become a schoolboys heaven. I loved every part of this hectic scene and vowed never to miss a single outing if I could avoid it and there were to be many such trips over my teenage years.

Once on the road again we steamed for home with only about 3 miles to go now. After passing through Minskip I swung the iron wheel to the right as we entered the home stretch. The road here was quite narrow so I had to be very careful and the hedges were very close to the road edge making visibility difficult even from our elevated driving position. We were soon thundering up our village street, much to the amazement of the locals, and came to a hissing halt in front of the royal oak pub. As usual James had a massive thirst on and nothing less than a few pints of William Younger's Best bitter was likely to quench it. As he entered the bar I was engulfed by kids and adults alike all coming out for a thorough inspection. 'Pride Of The Road' stood still in high distain until everyone had taken their fill of her. She seemed to revel in all the admiration and maybe a little jealousy. A few locals turned out with their old Kodak Brownie cameras for a quick snap of history.

I selected low gear and slowly edged the old girl forward with a few hoots and toots of the whistle. Carefully I crept up the short drive into our farmyard. I parked her up in a quiet corner of the yard between the stone barn and the fold yard before dropping the remains of the fire and cleaning out the ash pan. We had already found that the oil and grease was much easier to wipe off whilst still hot so I armed myself with a bundle of cotton waste and got stuck into it. Talking about a good clean up, boy, oh! Boy. Was I going to enjoy a good long soak in the bath to ease my aching joints and sore muscles. James wandered in to help me with the cleaning and he decided to leave the tarpaulin off until morning when all the metal would be cold.

Next up were my farm chores such as collecting and packing the day's eggs. Checking and feeding the animals and poultry before that longed for bath and a good feed. It was a major effort to get dressed and drag myself out to catch the bus, which fortunately stopped close to our front door.

Ballroom dancing had hitherto been my great love and passion, taking up most of my spare time and keeping me fit four nights per week. Over my life quite a few people, mainly men have scorned my love of ballroom dancing. I just ask them, "Can you tell me of any other way that you can enter a room full of lovely ladies and be quite certain to hold each one of them close in your arms before the night is over? If you go on your own to the cinema or theatre etc. it is almost certain that you would be hard pressed to even talk to a lady let alone chat with her during the evening and the same applies to a pub or bar especially if you were very self conscious as I was in those days. I expected to suffer a fair bit physically on this night due to my exertions during the day but once I got going to a good Quickstep beat I was ok. Fortunately, due to living on a small farm I was always very fit and strong for my age and size. It was going to take a fair amount of juggling from now on to fit my new hobby into the equation but most of our tractor trips would be in the summer whereas ballroom dancing was more of a winter entertainment. I was so looking forward to our next outing on the tractor. In the meantime of course there was the pressing need to rub down and repaint James's van to make it blend in with the tractor.

I always found ballroom dancing a bit of a challenge. In those days I was terribly self-conscious and I suppose it was the fear of rejection that bothered me. Even though I was a very competent dancer I always felt inferior and I could not believe that any girl or young lady would want to dance with me let alone go out with me on a steady date. After attending old time dancing classes two nights per week and becoming a very competent dancer I still felt that girls might refuse my offer to dance with them and I didn't want to face their rejection in front of others. I soon found out that it was senseless to try and dance with the "belles" of the ball. I often found these perfectly primped and preened young ladies were a big disappointment. For a start there was always lots of competition for their favours from more handsome and pushy young men than me. I also realised that most of them were not particularly nice to dance with. Their main concerns were their looks and coiffeurs, clothes and make-up. They insisted in dancing at arm's length so as not to mess up their dresses and make-up which I also felt was rude and insulting. If they felt like that about it maybe they should have refused my invitation and sat out the dance. In fact most of them were pains in the arse. They were so far up themselves that they were not nice to others. Therefore I tended to seek out the very nice but often not so glamorous girls who were happy to let themselves go a bit, cuddle up to their partner and dance so beautifully together, almost as one being.

On one occasion I went to the dance at our local town hall and enjoyed a number of dances with the girls that I knew would be more than happy to dance with me. I noticed a girl in a blue dress with white polka dots on it sitting in front of centre stage. She hadn't danced at all up to then. Why? She was very well dressed and quite beautiful and looked a nice happy girl. I eventually bucked up courage and asked her for the pleasure of dancing together and she gladly accepted. The young lady had attended the same dance the previous week with mixed results. She was a very competent dancer who had been taught by professionals and found it was very uncomfortable dancing with lesser exponents of dance so she rejected most offers to dance. It turned out that she had been watching my dancing skills as I perambulated around the hall with other girls and I had passed with flying colours. She was a magnificent dancer and I danced every dance with her for the rest of the evening.

I was hoping to further my acquaintance with my delightful partner but unfortunately she told me that she was only a visitor to our lovely town.

She lived in Scarborough a seaside town some 60miles away and was staying in our area because her parents had serious business commitments in Harrogate for a couple of weeks. She had to refuse my offer to see her safely home to her father's posh hotel in Harrogate but only because their chauffer had been instructed to collect her from outside the hall at midnight. Unfortunately I never met my fantastic dance partner again because she was due to return to Scarborough, miles away, within a few days.

I suppose these incidents highlighted the value of my life with "Pride Of The Road". She seemed quite happy to have me along as her partner and she never baulked at sharing her time with me. We had a fabulous time throughout my teenage years as we shook, rattled, and rolled around North Yorkshire and Lancashire together. She introduced me to lots of lovely people and fantastic scenery that I would never have got to know if I had not partnered up with her.

Oh yes we had our moments of worry and grief and she took more looking after than a kindergarten full of assorted kids but she was always there at the end of the road huffing and puffing contentedly as we rubbed her down and pulled the big tarpaulin over her.

Chapter 2

THE PICKERING RALLY

It was a very sad forlorn sight that I was faced with on a daily basis. Pride of the road covered up with a heavy-duty tarpaulin parked in the corner of our farmyard awaiting our next outing together. However there were a few moments of glory that were to cheer me up as the days went by.

The village was surrounded by an extensive gravel quarry and the company that ran it were always looking out for more deposits of this valuable commodity needed for building and renovating houses and factories. A new site was located close to the village church, but across the road from the main quarry, which held great promise but alas the deposit was infiltrated with a quantity of clay which was not easy or economical to wash out of the gravel causing the site to be abandoned. According to the laws of the time the site had to be renovated and revegetated after mining ceased. The mining company hired a bulldozer to spread out the surface soil which had been returned to the site. Because a large amount of gravel had been removed the surface level of the renovated ground was a fair bit lower than it had been originally. Once the dewatering ceased along with the mining operations, the underground water table was slowly rising to its former level. Unaware, the bulldozer driver pushed and shoved the top soil around for about a week until one afternoon it sank down onto it's belly and stayed there. A couple of local farmers were asked to help out with their tractors but the dozer was well stuck. At this point the driver came to see James to ask if he thought the steam tractor could extract his machine. Ever the optimist, James replied.

'Yea, of course, the old girl can move anything and we're willing to give it a go but it will be expensive especially if we have to use the winch.'

A suitable price was finally agreed to and the job was on. As it was Friday evening we decided to tackle the job in the morning provided the owners agreed to pay the costs. We removed the tarpaulin and lit the fire overnight to enable an early start next day. With the fire damped down for the night we retired to bed.

Saturday morning dawned bright and sunny so we got the tractor ready and as soon as we had a full head of steam we set off across the road to try our luck. There was a row of large mature sycamore trees along the fence line and within easy reach, so a large steel cable was wrapped around one of them and the free ends securely hitched to the towing hitch of our tractor. Then we ran out the winch cable that was coiled on a drum on the rear axle of the tractor and hitched it to the bulldozer. We thought that we could easily winch the dozer on to solid ground but it had sunk over night and was well and truly stuck. The tracks were almost covered with mud and when the blade was fully raised it was still digging into the ground. Most of the village people lined up along the fence to watch the spectacle as, slowly but surely the pressure of the winch inched the dozer out of the bog. The driver had the dozer tracks turning, trying to help but to little avail. It took us most of the morning to get the dozer on to firmer ground so that it could travel on it's own power. When we went to retrieve the cable from around the sycamore tree we realised that the tree was cut so very deeply that the tree would have to be felled for safety. We took the old girl home triumphantly, snorting and puffing up the drive ready for a good wash down before being put back in the corner of the yard for a long earned rest.

As time went by there were a number of small jobs around that needed the use of a machine like the tractor so we obliged where possible and the money earned was needed to keep the tractor in good condition and finance future trips to rally grounds. James always spent some of the money to build up a stock of steaming coal ready for a long trip when the need occurred.

The Pickering rally is now one of the finest in the country. It has grown to be a thrilling 3 day event with exhibits coming from all over Europe. When James first mentioned the event it was still in its infancy. It had begun a couple of years earlier in 1953 if my memory serves me well. It began when a number of local farmers decided to have a fun day out from their daily grind on the farms. They agreed to set up on Burtons field along Thornton road. The event was to be a few helter-skelter races around the field and a series of tug-of-war events between modern farm tractors and steam engines owned by local farmers. The day proved to be so successful that it became an annual event. This meant moving to a different location and a committee was set up to run it to raise funds for village amenities.

We were very keen to go to Pickering Rally in spite of the long journey by road on iron wheels, however there was one serious obstacle in the way. The Hambleton hills, which spring up off the plain of York near Easingwold and run in a more or less north-westerly direction to Osmotherly. They rise very suddenly and steeply off the plain up to the moors on the top. There were only very limited ways of scaling these hills from our end, at least, and without travelling all the way to York city we were left with the option of Sutton Bank or Wass bank. Each of these climbs was long and very formidable. They were each 3-4 miles up the steepest inclines and the worst gradients were 1 in 4 and 1 in 5 with nasty vicious hairpin bends thrown in for good measure. We were not at all concerned with the tractor's power and ability to scale these hills. The problem lay in the fact that the boiler was designed to operate horizontally. When the boiler was inclined either way the water level indicators were useless so we would have to guess the water level once we left the plain. This was a common occurrence in all our travels but most hills were only relatively short so as long as we kept the water level correct whilst on the flat we could cope with the incline. If there was too much water in the boiler at any one time there was the real danger of sucking enough of it into the piston cylinder and exploding the end cover off the cylinder. On the other hand if there was insufficient water the boiler could overheat and melt the safety plug letting water flow onto the fire. Imagine what a disaster that would be. If either of these scenarios eventuated we would have been immobilised for a long time and stuck on that steep narrow road causing a serious obstruction in an area that was difficult enough anyway. Neither of the route options were very favourable but we had to select the easiest and hope we got it right first time.

Well there you go: it only took half a dozen cups of tea to resolve the obvious. We decided to cut across country and tackle Wass bank rather than Sutton bank. This meant that we only had to travel a short distance beyond Boroughbridge and Langthorpe on the A1 highway then we could turn off to our right and run on byroads across the plain of York.

As per usual James and I gathered up our necessities such as tools, coal and wet weather gear during the week ready for a quick getaway early on Saturday morning. We were ready to travel just after daylight and as we meandered down the village street James slowed down and stopped outside his parents bakery to load up with fresh bread numerous pies and assorted cakes to set us straight for the day. Boroughbridge was only a couple of miles away but it was situated on the dreaded A1 highway. Getting through this old coaching town was never a pleasure with it's extremely narrow streets, stone bridges and always lots of activity. However, provided we approached it with caution it didn't delay us very much at all. Once we crossed the river Ure and swung around into Langthorpe we only had to turn off to our right heading for Brafferton and Helperby. There were no really suitable direct roads heading for wass so after about 4 miles we had to dogleg to our right into Brafferton village and the adjoining Helperby village where we turned off to our left towards Raskelf. About half a mile before Raskelf village we turned left again. After less than a mile we zigzagged across the A19 highway. Water was no problem at all for once. There were lots of little becks and streams situated along the roadside for our convenience. Once across the A19 it was only about 6 miles from Wass village. Our journey took us through the lovely scenic villages of Hustwaite and Coxwold then skirting past the ruins of Byland Abbey and into Wass village. All along this scenic drive we were in awe of the idyllic natural beauty of the countryside which is interspaced with historic farm homesteads, unbelievably beautiful villages and ancient ruins of the middle ages.

As we travelled along we got glimpses and good views from time to time, of the White Horse of Kilburn. This is quite a spectacle, carved into the chalk cliffs on the near vertical face of the Hambleton Hills. Back in the mid eighteen hundreds the local schoolteacher along with a couple of dozen helpers cleared the vegetation and sculpted this unusual sight after copying a similar horse near Uffington in Berkshire. The sculpture is about 230 feet tall and 310 feet long and can be seen many miles away across the plain of York. I lived in a cottage on a farm near Grafton most of my young life and I could clearly see the White Horse from our back yard. It must have been 12 to 15 miles away across the river and fields but it stood out dramatically on the hillside.

Although it was a full time job driving the tractor we were travelling so slowly that we were able to have a good long look at the beautiful vistas as we rolled along. Standing high up on the tractor platform we had a good view of things that we had no hope of ever seeing from the seat of a speeding car. There can be no doubt about it that this part of North Yorkshire is truly magnificent. We were rolling along with the weak, early, sunshine glowing through between the fluffy white clouds and warming our bodies promising a lovely spring day. We had originally planned to arrive near Byland Abbey in time for morning tea in that loveliest of settings but we were running a bit late and James had a better idea. As we entered the village of Coxwold James turned to me and stated, 'Brian, this is a delightful village with beautiful, historic buildings all the way through it. What do you say if we stop in front of one of them, top up the water from the beck, and enjoy our break in this gorgeous place?'

'Sounds great to me pal.' I replied. 'I don't suppose the building you have in mind has a sign out the front with 'Fauconberg Arms' carved on it by any chance?'

'Hey pal, you're a bit of a genius, I would never have considered that particular one but it's your fault that we're so late and it's just after opening time already so it will have to do and I have to keep up the enginemen's code as well.'

'You are trying to tell me that you are duty bound to taste and test the ale in this hostelery so that you can discuss the quality of it with other steam engine drivers who might be lucky enough to be passing through this village.' I retorted.

'Aye well, now you come to mention it, that just might be my duty an' all. There you are I said you were a genius and you go and prove it.' James replied as he slowed down for me to turn across into the tiny little parking area out in front.

After only a couple of pints of best bitter James declared it fit to drink so we set off once again for Wass village and that awful hill beyond.

James suggested that the historic town of Helmsley would make a suitable lunch stop leaving us a nice run over the moors during the afternoon providing we managed to negotiate the long hard road out of the valley onto the moor top.

As we left the village it was clearly obvious that we were already climbing steadily towards the main hill. With a fair amount of experience behind us James decided to risk staying in top gear as much as possible. The longer we were on the slope the more likely the chance of getting the water level wrong and causing some serious damage. As it was we were likely to be on the steep incline for at least an hour and maybe more. James opened up the throttle valve wide and we were soon travelling close to our full speed of about 12 miles per hour. About halfway up the hill we found a run off onto the moor which we could use to gain a level check point for the boiler. We drove just past the run off then James carefully eased us backwards and I spun the steering wheel around to our left.

James called out, 'I hope the ground here is solid enough to carry our weight or we are in serious trouble, I'll ease her along the track and if you think we are sinking in give me a shout.'

I needed eyes in my backside to watch everything but the ground was very firm from constant use over many years. Once James felt that we were standing pretty level he shut off the engine whilst we checked the water levels. We had used a fair bit more water than expected but not seriously so. The steam pump soon had the level back up to the gauge top and the fire was roaring away to get maximum steam for the next assent. James had oiled everything insight and we were off again but this time in low gear. James was much happier now because the stop had allowed us to get some idea how much water we were using each mile. The tractor seemed to revel in the challenge and settled down to the task quite happily and before we knew it we crested the ridge and pulled up onto a flat area of grass just off the road. It was now necessary to check each part of the motion and every bearing as we topped up the water in the boiler and added more coal to the fire. James added oil to the oilers as he checked around and I organised a mug of tea each and some chunks of toast from the firebox. The scenery up here was truly magnificent and we sat in the tough moorland grass to enjoy our simple meal with a stiff breeze in our hair and the sun shining down on our backs.

James was soon eager to be off again as we still had lots of hard work ahead of us. The tractor rolled comfortably along the A170 highway and ran close by Sproxton before cruising down hill towards Helmsley, a beautiful town snuggled comfortably in a deep hollow among the moorland. The stark remains of the castle keep pointed skywards from it's carefully manicured lawns guiding us towards the town. Both of us were very familiar with this stretch of road and the towns and villages interspersed along it but this day we were not here to revel in it's glory only to pass on through. Sadly our itinerary didn't allow us the ultimate pleasure of exploring the secluded dales to the north of our passage. Included in these are Farndale with its carpets of daffodils in the spring, Bransdale tucked away in a corner, then Rosedale in all its glory and finally Newtondale mainly accessible only by the moors railway and flowing right into Pickering itself.

Everywhere we went we were treated as celebrities and Helmsley was no exception. Much to everyone's pleasure we decided to make it our lunch stop. James selected a lovely public house that dispensed his favourite brew of ale to which he added a famous brand of pork pies and we were all set. Tourists and locals alike swarmed around us asking so many questions about the tractor, its history and our travels. The publican of that little pub must have prayed for us to stay around all day. The bars were full and the beer garden overflowing throughout our stay. However all good things must end and we still had about 12miles to negotiate before we could rest ourselves and the tractor. The organising committee had arranged for us to park up on a farm quite close to the rally ground so it was soon time to move off again. Our next objective was the town of Kirbymoorside which lay almost halfway between Helmsley and Pickering. Here was another of these beautiful windswept Yorkshire towns carefully folded into the landscape safe and secure. At this point the tractor needed little attention other than a few squirts of oil and a quick drink from the local beck. Then it was back onto the road for the final few miles. We easily found the farm where the tractor was to be billeted and moved slowly into the farmyard. The owners appeared from the milking parlour where they had just finished milking.

We jumped down and exchanged warm greetings before the tractor had to be thoroughly inspected by our hosts. We were shown where to park the old girl then went through our usual shutdown procedure. At this point we were only about 15 miles short of the show ground so for once we had a little time on our hands to have a look round the farm and the stupendous views around about. We pitched in with the farm and household chores until it was time to head into the huge bathroom for a jolly good scrub down in time to eat another glorious home cooked farm meal. Our hosts were very genial and we all enjoyed a good old chinwag before heading to bed.

Next morning it was "all hands to the wheel" to get everything ready for the trip into town. Our hosts were coming along with us as soon as all the farm chores had been attended to. Travelling 10 or 15 miles was old hat to us now and the tractor was in fine fettle. It was a glorious north Yorkshire morning with sun shining in our faces as we rolled comfortably along the road. We encountered very little traffic along the way and were soon in the rally ground polishing and preening the tractor ready for the judges. Once the judging was over and the best dressed engines in each category had been chosen the fun began. A series of crazy races was organised including barrel racing across the field. Swinging that huge cast iron wheel from lock to lock was sheer bloody murder. It took about 18 turns to get from one full lock to the other and after more than a dozen of these we were absolutely knackered. Most of us were too stuffed to get down from the platform but everyone declared that we would do it again at the next rally.

After a great deal of fun frivolity and mateship everyone said their farewells and headed homewards. We went back to join our overnight hosts to help with the chores and park up the tractor until the following week.

The next weekend James picked me up early on the Saturday morning and I curled up on some sacks in the back of his old van so that Pat could have the passenger seat to herself and away we went. The drive to Pickering was splattered with heavy showers and rain so we were hoping that the old saying would come true today. It went something like this, "rain before seven fine before eleven." You would have to be pretty dumb to believe that sort of rot but we were due for a bit of good luck and sure enough by the time that we had the tarpaulin folded up a weak watery sun broke through the clouds to shine down on us as we lit the fire. We had a couple of hours to kill whilst the fire did it's job which we spent helping out on the farm. Our hosts provided us with a delicious morning tea party then we bade them farewell and hit the road.

Up on the moors traffic was light and slow so we were able to roll along quite fast on a decent road surface. There was no doubt in our minds that the tractor performed much better if driven close to top speed and steering it was a dream in comparison to 4 mph. We rolled sedately through Helmsley to much awe and admiration and stopped for lunch on a small flat piece of moorland grass at the very top of Sutton bank. Near where we were parked there is an unusual sculpture on the ground. My memory fails me yet again and for the life of me I cannot remember the history of it but it takes the form of a sort of maze. The ground has been cut away in a sort of pattern leaving a grass pathway curling in towards the centre. I understand that it is some sort of exorcism. The theory is that because the path curves sharply into the centre it wards off evil spirits as you walk around the circle. It is believed that evil spirits cannot easily turn around the continuous curves so by the time that you reach the centre your spirit is free of all impediments. I have never been able to work out why the evil spirits cannot just wait on the outside of the circle and hop back on when you exit the maze.

James had decided to risk Sutton bank hoping to save time and fuel. We were both aware of the problems and risks involved in this tricky manoeuvre but we thought we were clever enough to pull it off. The first descent was at 1in5 gradient so the boiler was as full as we dared to run it but if we sucked some water into the steam pipe it would smash up the engine cylinder. There was no way we were going to be able to check the boiler water level until we were on level ground some 3-4 miles away. James set the steam pump going steadily to try and keep the level up to the boiler head. The problem was that all the water ran to the front of the boiler but the firebox was at the rear. In the crown of the boiler firebox there was a special plug filled with a lead insert which was designed to melt and protect the boiler from overheating by allowing water to cascade down onto the fire and extinguish the flames. Once over the edge of that awesome drop the water level gauge was useless,(it only gave a true reading on level ground).

James put the tractor into gear and I swung the steering wheel to get us back onto the road, "Are you all set, pal he called out? We pulled the whistle chain and away we went."

The first descent was a straight piece of road running along besides the cliff then there was a very tight hairpin bend which turned us back alongside the cliff in the opposite direction. There was a sheer cliff face on our left hand side running back to the top of the moor and a sheer drop onto the valley floor to our right. Once around the hairpin the gradient increased sharply to 1in4 but the steam pressure was holding the tractor steady as we descended. We were getting quite cocky with ourselves as we neared the next sharp bend when all hell broke loose. There was a huge roar of steam as a jet of water hit the fire. We were totally engulfed in a storm of steam, ashes and smoke. It was unbelievable. Everything disappeared in the clouds of muck and gasses. We were on a steep descent with no brakes to speak of. The parking brake was no use here and the only other way to hold the tractor back was to hold it with the steam pressure but we had just lost all our steam. Now we were in serious trouble and there was still a long way to go before we got onto level ground. Suddenly, through all the steam smoke and ash I spotted a service track on our left heading out on to the moor that the rangers used in case of fires etc. The track, what little I saw of it, curved away from the roadside to our left and then began to go uphill onto the heather. I instinctively spun the steering wheel as hard as I could hoping that the ground along the track would hold the weight of the tractor (about 10 tonnes). Even getting badly bogged up here was many times better than hurtling down that awful hill and almost certainly rolling over at the bottom.

The tractor slowed and stopped going uphill then began to roll back towards the road so James reached for the parking brake, which he managed to screw down as we rolled back and forth in the hollow between the road and the moor.

"Damn and blast". James shouted out, "I never expected all that mess". Then he looked at me a burst into laughter. I was very shaken and quite upset and could see no humour in our predicament until James pointed to my face and clothes. I was in an unbelievable mess. "You should see the state your in me old pal"

I replied, "Heck James don't laugh too much until you see your face, it's never a pretty sight at best but now you look gastly. So saying I climbed down onto the grass to swill some water from the bunker tanks to clean myself up a bit. James joined me in my ablutions then he turned to me and asked. "How the hell did you know about that service track? I couldn't even see the flywheel let alone a cart track across the moors."

"How the heck would I know," James I said. "The steam cleared a bit and I 'appened to be looking in that direction as the track appeared so I took a chance that the old girl wouldn't tip over, swung the wheel and hung on for grim death. Maybe the exorcism at the maze brought us good luck after all."

"Aye well pal I'm right glad you did. Rolling on her side would be miles better than hurtling down that dammed hill. So what the hell are we going to do now then."

"I suppose we'll 'ave to wait until the firebox cools down remove the ash pan and get the fire bars out so you can get in and replace the fusible plug. You have a spare plug in the toolbox 'avent you."

"Oh hell! Yea there's a plug in there alright but I never got around to refilling it with new lead."

"I suppose there's a blacksmith or plumber in Kilburn village where we can refill it but it's a long walk there and back unless you can get a lift." I replied.

"Oh little smart arse aren't you. What makes you think I'm going to walk all that way then? What about you doing the walking?

"Well it's your fault the plug wasn't refilled and anyway I reckon I've thought of a better way to get the tractor going again."

"Oh yea, quite a little smarty pants today aren't we? So tell me clever dick what have you come up with then?"

"Well I was just thinking. That fire hole door is a

fair bit bigger than the bobhole (the little doorway that the hens use) to enter our hen house."

"What the hell have old 'ens and hen houses got to do with a tractor then? You tell me that young man." James enquired.

"Well it's like this you see James, my shoulders are very narrow and I can climb in and out of our 'en 'ouses quite easily so there! I reckon I can crawl into the firebox once it cools down enough. We can line the fire bars with layers of our firewood and some wet heather and empty coal sacks then I can crawl in the box with the big stillson wrench and change the plug whilst you go for a little walk. Whilst you're away I can fill the bucket out of that little stream near the road and use it to start refilling the bunker tank. We'll need a hand pump or stirrup pump and a hose pipe whilst your at it to top up the boiler again. See if you can borrow one on your travels. I bet that will be a lot quicker and easier than dropping the ash pan and pulling the fire bars out off the bottom of the firebox"

"Ok smartypants I do the work as usual whilst you just lie on your back" James replied as he headed off down the hill towards the village muttering and mumbling obscenities as he went whilst I topped up the water tanks after laying the sacks in the stream. There was a reducing elbow and funnel in the tool box so I screwed the filler plug out of the boiler side to see if I could pour enough water in to the boiler to light the fire again. I found out that it was possible but would be slow and arduous but what the heck I had nothing better to do for a long time yet.

I was able to top up the bunker then set about filling the boiler. I was able to fill it up to the point that the water ran out of the fusible plug hole before James got back. He had managed a lift into the village and the driver was so intrigued that he drove him back again also bringing with them a stirrup pump borrowed from the blacksmith who had repaired the plug. I had continued to overfill the boiler for a while because the water spilling down from the plug was cooling the fire bars and the ash pan.

Once James returned I laid all the sacks and heather into the firebox then very carefully crawled in after soaking my clothes with water. Everything was still quite hot and steamy so I needed great care not to burn myself. Once the new plug was in place James and his new friend pumped the boiler up with enough water whilst I relit the fire. We had a bit of food whilst we waited so we could get cracking as soon as possible. We had lost a lot of time and there wasn't too much daylight left by the time that we had enough steam to travel again. We made a quick trip to the blacksmith's shop to return the pump and set off for home once more.

James decided that we had had enough of roughing it on rural roads so he told me to stay on the A170 and steer towards the town of Thirsk. We needed to find an overnight camp site somewhere around Thirsk which was only about 6 or 7 miles away and close enough for us to bypass via Sowerby and onto the A168 towards Dishforth. We had a good run into the town and met only a minimum of traffic on the way through. Once on the A168 we seriously began to hunt for a camp site and whilst we were refilling the water tanks at a nearby beck a curious farmer walked onto the road to check us out. The fellow was enthralled with the tractor and offered to let us camp in his yard nearby. His family rushed out to see us negotiate the driveway. There were 3 boys and the prettiest little girl you could imagine. She was about 3 years old and full of life. The boys were all in primary school and were soon crawling all over the tractor. They insisted on helping us so James gave them an oil can apiece and stood back to watch them. The whole process was a bit messy but what the heck? You only live once.

Once the shutdown was complete we went inside for a good clean up and a delicious meal. The people apologised that they had no spare room for us to sleep but we told them that we were quite happy to camp in our sleeping bags amongst the hay in the big barn.

I crawled out next morning about daybreak and after a good swill in the cattle trough I went over to check the tractor and stoke up the fire. When we had good quality coal the fire went well all night with very little slate and slag so it took only a stir up with the poker and a top up with fresh fuel. The kids were out and about shortly after I was and insisted that they "help" me get the tractor ready. I gave them each a bundle of cotton waste to do some cleaning and polishing. That kept them all quiet and out of the way whilst I restocked the coalbunker. The farmer's wife called us in to the kitchen for a feed of bacon and eggs washed down with lots of tea. Once again this grand Yorkshire hospitality left us in total awe of these lovely people. The kids all piled on top of the coalbunker for a quick ride around the stack yard and out onto the road. We had to assure our hosts that any time we were nearby we would visit them and why would we not. Then we were on our way home at last with everyone waving and shouting madly.

The A168 took us through Topcliffe and Asenby then on to Dishforth where we turned onto the A1 highway for the run to Boroughbridge. Fortunately the A1 was reasonably quiet so we were able to scoot along at a good old pace. We picked up enough water at Kirbyhill to get us home. James was pleased to see that the Royal Oak was still open for business as we pulled into our yard. After the usual shut down procedure we put the old girl to bed until the following weekend.

Chapter 3

OVER THE MOUNTAINS

It was a bitterly cold winter's afternoon and as I stepped off the west Yorkshire bus on my way home from school, a gusty north east wind grabbed my over coat and screamed through my bones. Winter had settled in with a vengeance, the penalty for living in North Yorkshire. The northeast wind boded ill. That is the direction from which frost and snow were likely to come. I hurried across the road into our yard dreading having to spend the next two hours or so feeding our live stock and collecting the days eggs ready for packing into boxes for market. Suddenly a face bearing a cheesy grin appeared from the doorway of the blacksmith shop and James Alderton called out to me, "I'm right busy just now young man but I need to have a bit of a talk to you. Can you come on over after your tea 'cause we 'ave a fair bit to sort out if you see."

"Aye, right you are then James I'll be there about 7.30 if that's ok with you." I replied.

I was a bit surprised at James's summons because it was the wrong season for any tractor journeys but, when dealing with our local plumber one never could tell which way he would jump next. Tractor journeys were a summer treat and ballroom dancing was for winter evenings.

Once the dishes were washed and put away I headed over the road to see James. It was good to step into their living room out of the biting wind. The slow combustion stove was stacked up with coke and the kettle boiling it's head off. Once I was armed with a cup of steaming cocoa James pushed a copy of the World's Fair newspaper under my nose and pointed out and article in the wanted column. The University of Manchester was advertising for a fleet of steam powered vehicles to haul their carnival tableaux around their city streets to raise money for charity. Every year the various departments of the university decorated lorries with an assortment of amusing and entertaining themes such as nursery rhymes etc. On a predetermined

Tuesday the lorries set off on a circular tour of the city centre collecting thousands of pounds in donations from a grateful populace.

This year the university was faced with cancelling the event because of the Suez war in Egypt. The Suez canal had been closed due to the war and a number of sunken ships were blocking this vital world trade link. Most of the world's fuel oil supplies were east of the blockage meaning that all the shipping was forced to use the long way around. The journey down the east African coast, around the Cape of Good Hope and back up the west coast of Africa added many days sailing for the tankers carrying our fuel supplies and of course all our other shipping. The shortage of fuel oil had forced the British government to severely ration all fuel so they could direct supplies to essential industries to keep the country running. All non-essential use of fuel, especially diesel was cancelled for the duration and of course that included the carnivals and fairground rides as well.

"So James," I asked "How does this advert affect us? You're surely not suggesting that we head off to Manchester are you? The cost of coal alone will break you. Then there are all the other expenses along the way and a week off work. It must be all of 60 or 70 miles each way."

"Aye well, your right about all that stuff but 'ave a look at this letter. You see, Pat wrote to the university in reply to that advertisement and this is what came back."

So saying he handed me a letter from the Chemistry Department of the university acknowledging our response and offering to pay all reasonable expenses for fuel, accommodation and meals if we were prepared to tackle the journey. They went on to say that it would assist them greatly if we could locate a suitable 4 wheeled trailer and bring it along too.

"Hey, James," I said, "I've just remembered! There's a large trailer up at Stubbing's barn that's only used at harvest time. I'll skid over to Tippet's place on my bike in the morning and ask if we can borrow it."

"Heck, that's really great, Brian. Do you think old Fred will let us borrow it?"

"I can't see why not, it's only parked out in the weather. We would have to clean it up and grease the wheel bearings and other joints but that won't take long. They'll probably tow it down here with one of their tractors next time they come through." I replied.

"Ok, that's settled then. I'll leave you to organise summat with Fred. It'll be right 'andy 'cause we can carry most of our coal and tools on there out of our way." James answered. We chatted on for a while before I had to brave the elements again, leave the fire and run home across the road.

On Saturday morning I hopped on my bike and headed for the Tippet farm which was a mile or two on the road to Ripon. I met my friend Eric in the barnyard and asked him about the four-wheel cart up at Stubbing's barn.

"Oh heck you needn't bother to ask Brian. Dad won't mind at all and we won't need it 'til next harvest time. Hey pal, I've just remembered, we have to run down to Tollerton early in the morning to collect the threshing drum. I'll get our Frank to drop it off for you. Come on, give me a hand to start the old Massey Harris tractor then we can bring the cart down here nice and handy for him."

Once the tractor was going we headed up the tortuous track through the ford in the beck and up to Stubbing's barn. There we hooked up the cart and pulled it back to the house yard ready for Frank in the morning. I was feeding our pigs the following morning when I heard the tractor slowing down before turning into our yard. I showed Frank where to park the cart so that I could jack it up to remove each wheel in turn. The wheels needed to be taken off to clean and regrease the axles and adjust any slack and wear. I spent most of the day greasing the springs and the turntable as well as the wheel bearings. I had to replace some boards on the tray top to repair a couple of holes. By the time that I caught up with James at the end of the day it was more or less ready for the road.

James called in when he returned home from a big plumbing job and was surprised to see the cart in the yard. "By heck pal. You 'aven't wasted any time 'ave you. That looks great. Do we need to do anything to it before a long trip to Manchester?"

"No James, not now anyway. I've been right through it and it's ready to go. I did think that you might want to get me a tin of red paint to match the colour of the engine then I can paint the framework so it will look respectable in the parade."

"By heck, your quite right there it does look a bit

scruffy and we can give it a rub with a wire brush then a couple of coats of that Marshall Red paint. I 'ave to go into Harrogate on Monday for a little job so I'll see to it for you. I'll get us a couple of new wire brushes and some paint brushes, that'll do the trick. By I'm right chuffed with you Brian. We 'aven't much time to get everything ready and this weather is keeping me on the run at present so I'll 'ave to lean on you a fair bit if that's ok."

"Yea that's ok pal. We've lots of old engine oil round the back of the shed so tomorrow I'll slop a heap of it onto the floorboards so it will soak in before next weekend then we can start loading the bags of coal." I said.

"Aye well it seems you've gotten things sorted out so I'll leave you to look after everything, if that's ok with you." James replied as he was leaving.

Sunday dawned bright and clear so I got out the drum of sump oil and an old broom. I more or less tipped the oil from the drum and spread it out roughly with the broom and left it to soak into the old badly weathered floorboards. Next it was out with the wire brush to remove the faded or flaking paint from the wooden frame and the steel drawbar. The wheels needed many hours of scrubbing before I could begin to paint them. I only had a few evenings and the next weekend to get the painting done. I had some help from my friends in the village and a little from James. The following weekend James and Pat pitched in to help and by Sunday evening all was spick and span. Fred tippet was going to get a shock when we returned the cart after the trip.

With only one more week to go we had to spend all our free time rounding up all the bits and pieces needed for the trip. It was a little hard because we had no itinerary as such. Most of the road was strange to us and we had no idea how difficult or easy it would be to get water and find places to stop over night and over a week. It was going to take us two long weekends of hard driving to get there on time. Late on Friday evening we lit the fire and banked it up over night so that we could leave at daylight. The days were much shorter in the depths of winter so every second was precious. All our coal, tools and camping gear were loaded ready to go. I wasn't looking forward to the prospect of camping out at this time of year but we might be lucky although the forecast was gloomy.

Before daybreak I rode my bike down the

village to get fresh bread for breakfast and some to take with us. James parents were the local bakers so I got fresh hot bread and Mrs Alderton put in a box of assorted cakes and fruit pies for our snacks. Back at the tractor the fire was roaring away so I toasted a large slab of bread in the fire box door. I was sitting on the platform munching toast and washing it down with scalding hot tea when James and Pat arrived. "I 'ope you've got some of that for me pal it smells so good."

"Aye I 'ave that James and your tea's ready an' all." I replied. One last check around and we were off down the village heading for Knaresborough town on the road to Wetherby. The road was relatively quiet this early and no coppers about so we made very good time. There was a short steep hill alongside the golf club to descend as we approached Knaresborough and as the first houses appeared I turned off to our left into chain lane which ran along the bottom of the town and joined up with halfpenny lane near the railway line thus avoiding having to negotiate the main street traffic and the steep hills along it. We came to the main road to York, which we had to enter then cross over onto the road to Wetherby. The

Wetherby road meandered through the lovely village of Little Ribston and on to our first water stop near Wetherby.

There was a handy stream with enough room to park alongside it just before driving on to the Great North Road so we filled up the bunker tanks. A friend had donated some old 44 gallon drums for the trip. They were nearly rusted out but he thought they might help by keeping us going at places where there was limited or no water available. We had a siphon hose with us so we could empty them without stopping in traffic if needs be. We had decided to reserve this supply of water for use in emergencies so we needed to fill up the bunker at each available supply. We had to stop and oil all the bearings and slides every few miles anyway so James attended to the oil can whilst I sucked up the water. As I climbed back on board James asked, "What do you reckon about this weather Brian? I don't like the look of it at all and I'm frozen stiff standing here beside you with nothing energetic to do to keep my blood circulating"

"At least wrestling with the steering wheel is keeping me a bit warmer but it's very cold and the wind's in the north east again. I don't like it very much at all and my hands are freezing hanging onto this iron wheel but we have to press on or run out of time." I replied

"Well that's true enough, pal, so here we go again. Stick your hand out and give the whistle a good toot." We moved off out into the traffic again and headed into town. Most of the town businesses were located off the highway to our right so our passage was quite smooth. The Great North Road runs right through the centre of the town and it is extremely narrow. Just a short way beyond the town we had to turn right onto the Leeds road where the traffic was fairly heavy. In those days all commercial vehicles were restricted to 30 miles per hour and all heavy lorries to 20 miles per hour so our speed wasn't as annoying as it would be today. At times we were running along at 10 or 12 mph. It was much more pleasant to ride on at that speed because the wheel strakes just rolled smoothly over the tarmac making a mockery of the 4 mph speed limit. Even the steering was much easier and steadier at speed. We were also convinced that we used a fair bit less coal and water at the higher speeds.

About half an hour later a sudden flurry of wind had us concerned and then there was a noticeable temperature rise. These were sure indications that we might get a snow fall before nightfall. The sky was leaden with heavy black clouds and it was already getting dark. We took the bypass around Leeds city then turned off the roundabout onto the Huddersfield road. By then we were nithered (frozen stiff). Our fingers were icy cold and beginning to hurt. All the controls were solid iron and steel which soaked up all the heat from our fingers. Shortly after leaving the roundabout James declared that he had suffered enough so we started to look around for somewhere safe to park the tractor. It had already begun to snow quite heavily when I spotted a narrow lane leading off the main road and running behind a short row of cottages. It was a dead end street that had become cut off due to the road works on the bypass. The narrow alley opened up into a fairly large area of more-or-less desolate ground with plenty of room to turn our rig around and park up beneath a couple of trees. We stopped under the trees and jumped down for a council of war. James was quite sure that if we got off to a good start and all went well we could easily reach Manchester the following weekend. I commented, "What are you saying then James? Are you suggesting that we abandon the tractor and come back next Saturday and try again?"

"Aye well I don't see how we could do owt else." James replied. "I reckon we can make Huddersfield next Saturday and run over the Pennines into Oldham on Sunday. We can't possibly go on today. It'll be too dangerous 'cause we can hardly see where we're going and it's getting too dark to travel anyway. We'll have to park up soon and get back home. We can get the train from Leeds station to Harrogate then the bus home if we stop here so what do you reckon?"

"Ok you've convinced me. My fingers are hurting like hell and my nose is frozen. The big worry is will the engine still be here and will all the brass work still be on it when we get back? Even the stock of coal and the tools were at risk as we were on the outskirts of a big industrial city instead of a small village as planned".

We were still unresolved and continuing to warm ourselves on the firebox when a young lad of about 12 or thirteen years old wandered over. His eyes were all agog as he surveyed this monster quietly hissing steam and looking somewhat alien. He scratched his head beneath his cap then said with some authority.

"Now then you lads what 'ave we 'ere then? What are you doing with that tractor in our street?"

James answered the lad saying. "Well look 'ere young'un, it's like this you see, We 'ave to find somewhere safe to park this valuable tractor until next Saturday. You see, all that coal on t'cart and all the brass on the tractor are expensive and we 'ave to get to Manchester next weekend."

The lad said as cocky as you like. "Aye well mister you couldn't 'ave come to a better place. You can see there's plenty of room around 'ere and it's out o'way. Now it'll cost you a bob (shilling), or two but I can look after it for you. I'll make sure that nobody touches it or goes near it until you get back."

James was far from sure but he countered with, "Aye well I've got a ten bob note 'ere will that sort it out then?"

Quick as a flash the lad answered, "Oh aye, well if that's all you've got it'll do right enough.

Just then a voice called out, "Now then our

Wesley that's quite enough of your damned cheek."

The lady was a Mrs Johnston who said they lived in the house close to the front of the tractor. James had a chat with her and told of our predicament. "Oh that's alright then you can rely on our Wes. to look after your tractor, 'e rules the roost around 'ere and 'e won't stand any nonsense from nobody. He'll look after your tractor for you alright and if he earns a few bob that will be ok but not now."

Wesley gave us a hand to draw the fire and pack up our gear. We transferred as much coal as we could fit into the bunker and made everything else as safe as possible. The engine was still too hot to put the tarpaulin on when Mrs Johnson came out again and invited us into her home to warm our bones and get some hot homemade soup into us. That of course was just what we needed so we obliged the lady. James slipped some loose change into Wesley's hand for his help and promised the ten bob next weekend.

After our warm up and soup we tarped up the engine and prepared to depart. Wesley put his hand on James arm and seriously said. "Eh you don't 'ave to worry mister the old girl is in safe hands. I told you I'll look after 'er for you you'll damned well see I will, okay then."

James thanked Wesley who showed us to the nearest bus stop and waited to make sure we got on the right bus to get us to the railway station. By then it was snowing steadily and everything was rapidly turning white. At the station we boarded a train for the twenty mile journey to Harrogate where we had plenty of time for a mug of tea in the station cafeteria prior to catching the bus home. It was dark and bitterly cold by the time we reached the village. Mam and Dad were anxious to know what had happened and enjoyed the story about Wesley.

It was Tuesday evening before I caught up with James for a chat about the trip. He was a bit worried about our time schedule. We were cutting it very fine and didn't want to let the students down. I suggested that I could reverse our train and bus trip on Friday afternoon then I could prepare the tractor for the road. If I lit the fire and banked it down over night we could save a couple of hours at least. I offered to take my kit bag to school on Friday morning then leave from Knaresborough straight after classes finished.

"Aye well that 'ud be great lad." James said, "But you need somewhere warm to sleep. It will be freezing over night,"

"All my camping kit is on the trailer so I can make a bed alongside the fire box under the tarpaulin. It will be quite cosy under there. All I need to do is open up the tarp clear of the fire, in fact if I undo the tarp and turn it round so that it lies across the engine clear of the fire box it will reach to ground on both sides and make a nice cosy tent." I replied.

"Well I reckon your bloody mad" James retorted. "But it might work out. I tell you what, we'll 'ave a good look at t'weather report and get some idea what's going to "appen. If t'weather's going to be bad we won't be going at all. I'll just ring the university and say we can't make it, then we can recover the engine at any time. Right oh then, we'll leave it at then and see what the weekend forecast looks like on Thursday night,"

"Right you are then James I'll say goodnight for now and 'ope for a fine weekend." I answered.

We had a discussion about the weather as planned and the forecast looked quite good but there was the possibility of some rain showers.

We still decided to go to Manchester anyway. A few rain showers weren't going to stop us going providing the tractor was safe with Wesley. On Friday morning I only told Mam that we were leaving straight after school but "forgot" to mention camping out. My last two classes were only games periods and after a quick sob story to my teacher I was allowed to leave early. The trip to Leeds was straight forward and I got to the tractor in good time. I checked it over and found everything was in order before Wes appeared.

"Now then Brian what's to do. I reckoned you'd come early in the morning. Wes called out.

"Aye well we've a long way to go and we need to be away as soon as it's light enough to travel. I need to get steam up over night because it takes a couple of hours minimum." I replied. "Is tha' going to stop talking and give me a hand or is tha' busy like?"

"Aye, I am that I'll just pop in and tell our Mam what's 'appening. Are you going to spend all night on the tractor, or what?"

"I'll camp underneath next to the fire. I'll be as warm as toast. We'll cook our breakfast in the fire box in the morning then we'll be away." I answered.

"Aye, right you are I'll go and tell our Mam." Wes commented.

I was fastening the tarp down, having turned it and made it safe when Wes reappeared with his Mam. "Now then Brian, What's all this nonsense about you sleeping out 'ere then? As soon as you've got your fire going you come on in and get some hot soup into you and I'll get the spare bed aired ready for you. I'm not 'aving you sleeping outside at this time of year. Whatever are you thinking of?" She admonished me. "You'll catch your death of cold."

"Gosh that'll be very nice thankyou, Mrs Johnston, but I've got to be out very early in the morning to get steam up and I don't want to wake you up. I replied.

"Aye well you can think nowt about all that young man I allus gets up early any road and you can come and go as you please." She retorted.

There was no point arguing with this lady so that was settled.

Wes and I soon had a healthy fire going and began feeding it first with wood then added coal until we had a sizeable fire roaring up the chimney. We went inside for a big bowl of delicious soup with lots of crusty bread followed by a plateful of sausages and eggs. After a bit of a chat she showed me my room and the bathroom then it was back to work. Wes and I worked on the tractor until I was satisfied that it would be ready in time then banked up the fire and went to bed. Mrs Johnson had loaned me an alarm clock but I didn't need it. I woke up very early whilst it was still pitch black and sneaked outside. The fire was fine and it only needed the poker to loosen up the coals before adding more coal. By the time I went back inside to gather up my belongings Mrs Johnston had steaming hot porridge ready and Wes joined me at the table

"I was beginning to think you would sleep all day and I would have all the work to do myself." I said to Wes.

"You needn't worry, pal, at least the tractor is still all there, and safe and sound. It won't take us long to get her going now that I'm on t'job. I've been polishing her all week and she looks right bonny again. So hurry up and finish your tea so we can get cracking." Wes retorted. It was still dark outside but dawn was almost upon us. Wes and I removed and folded up the tarp and loaded it onto the cart. We tidied up the stuff on the cart and fastened it down ready for off. Headlights suddenly shone into the alley and James jumped out of the van. His friend Alan had been dragged from his nice warm bed to act as chauffer and deliver him safely. James was a bit surprised to find we had a nice head of steam and were nearly ready to go. By the time that we'd had another mug of Mrs Johnston's tea inside us it was time to roll.

James turned to Wes and said, "Now then young man I owe you a few bob for your help, don't I?"

"Aye well, that's what we agreed, ten bob it were." Wes replied

"Aye that's right enough you've done a right good job 'ere so 'ere it is and a bit more as well and thank you very much for a job well done." James answered.

Just then Mrs Johnston pushed in and said, "Don't give the little begger all that money James he's made enough already?"

"Oh give over our Mam" Wesley said. "You didn't 'ave to tell on me." And he hung his head in shame.

"What's all this carryon then?" James asked.

Mrs Johnston piped up again and stated. "I

caught the little begger the other night. He's been charging all his pals and school mates a tanner (sixpence) a time to 'ave a look and stand on the platform. He must 'ave made a fortune already.

"Is that right young man?" James said very sternly.

Wes was still staring at the ground waiting for severe retribution when James said. "Aye and I suppose they did most of this polishing as well didn't they?"

Wes looked up at James with a very contrite look on his face, "Aye well that's right enough. They wanted to help with the polishing and 'all tha knows, but I told you I'd look after her and I did didn't I?"

James was trying hard to keep a stern look on his face as he said, "Aye lad you did that an all so 'ere's your money and thanks again. Now then Mrs Johnston we must owe you a fair few bob for the food and lodging."

"Nay damn me James it was a real treat for me. You see my old man's a long distance lorry driver and he's away a lot so we get a bit lonely, if you see what I mean. So get away with you or else you'll be late. We might even see you on the way back, eh."

"Right you are then we'll say goodbye and we will call in on the way back thanks.

I often wonder what happened to Wesley over the years. He was as bright as a button, and as cunning as a shithouse rat but oh so lovable. Did he become a great business tycoon, entrepreneur, or would his mischievous ways lead him into trouble and maybe a term of incarceration at Her Majesty's Convenience. I hope not the latter because he was a great kid and we were very fond of him.

So we were on he road again heading for Huddersfield. The weatherman suggested that there were a few showers around but as yet it was fine but cloudy. James opened the steam valve in high gear and set a cracking pace. If all went according to plan this should be an easy run before setting off up onto the Pennine mountains tomorrow. We rolled along with easy grace until we had to find water. There was a nice little beck beside the road, which was easily accessible to us. By the time that we were ready to move off again it was raining steadily. When we approached the outskirts of Huddersfield we were wet through and very cold. We searched everywhere but there was no sign of any water so I jumped off the platform and left James to steer whilst I rigged up the siphon hose from the water drums. Just then there was a metallic clang and a savage rattling started near the left hand rear wheel. James pulled into the kerb so that we could have a look around to find the cause of the problem. The metal brackets mounting the guard over the drive gears had vibrated and broken through so that the guard was rubbing on the gears.

"Damn, this is the last thing we need, and right here in town." James stated. "Hey Brian have a look in that big tool box there should be a fair bit of wire in there and we might be able to support it until we can get it fixed. We were wrestling with the guard but not very successfully when an elderly gentleman walked up with his little dog, a Yorkshire terrier in fact. The man stopped to inspect the tractor and as I said before she was a magnificent display of brute force, architecture and artistry. He asked what the problem was that was causing our distress. I explained to the gent all of our problems and I asked if he knew of any blacksmiths or engineers around the area who might be able to help with welding the brackets.

"Oh aye, I do that young man. You've picked t'right place to break down. If you can get going a bit you'll be right. He pointed down the street and said,

"Now look 'ere see, there's yon pub on corner about two streets away. You need to turn down there then take next right then take a left straight away. Halfway down road you'll see a break in 'ouses on right hand side. The front is set back from road and there's a petrol pump agin wall. T'old bloke'll be there, 'e allus is you see. You might "ave to shout out to get 'im but 'e can fix that real good you see."

I thanked the man for his help then called out to James. "Hey James that man with the dog says that a fellow around yon corner can weld that for us so long as we can get there."

"Right you are then pal it'll hold that far so let's give it a go." James said as he extracted himself from the rear wheel. We set off carefully and turned where the man said. The cart was difficult to manoeuvre in the narrow streets but soon we were parked alongside the front entrance to the workshop. We went inside and found the owner who said he would have a quick look at it for us.

When he had had a good look at our problem he said, "This might be your lucky day. If you get rid of the cart in the roadway then back the tractor in and around so that this wheel is as close to the doorway as you can I might be able to fix it. Only a couple of weeks ago I got one of them thar newfangled electric welders. If the leads are long enough I can prop up the guard and you fellows can hold it in place while I weld it without pulling it off. It'll take all day if we 'ave to get that bloody great wheel off and then it will be hard to weld the bracket in exactly the right place. If it's done on there it will fit ok. By the time we got the cart off the rain had stopped again and I swung the steering wheel madly to get the back end to screw around. It was going to be hard to get in there but as James rolled the tractor back and forth I wrestled with the steering wheel until we were close enough. Percy, the blacksmith managed to screw himself in and around the spokes whilst we supported the guard. The leads were only just long enough to reach but Percy soon had it welded. "That's stronger than it ever was because I've welded that extra gusset on as well. I tell you what lads, I'll go and cut two more gussets and weld 'em on t'other brackets as well just to make sure." Percy declared.

When he was finished James said, "I don't suppose there's anywhere around here where we can park up for the night. It's getting late and we're cold and wet through. We don't want to be tackling yon 'ill at this time o'day neither."

Percy thought for a minute then stated. "Look 'ere I'll tell you what to do. If you hitch up again you can go on down street turn to your right and go too far end of the road into a big gateway. Gates is allus open so you can just drive in and try to park out of way of lorries. It's me brothers yard see and he wont mind. If there's no one about just park up where you can 'cause our Fred'll probably be down pub by now. I'll be going down there when I knock off so I'll let 'im know." James thanked Percy and when he paid him he gave him a bit extra to buy a pint or two for himself and his brother. Just as we were about to depart James had a bright idea. He asked Percy if he knew of somewhere where we might get a bed and meal for the night. Percy told him, "If you walk across the road from the lorry yard, there's a boarding house opposite and old Margaret might be able to fix you up. She has a sign on gate so you can't miss it. At this time 'o year she's a bit quiet so she might be able to 'elp you lads."

The yard was ideal for us to park up so I set about getting the engine settled down for the night whilst James checked with the old lady. Margaret said she could help out but there was only one double bed so as long as we were happy to share we could stay, the night.

James came back with the good news and helped with the engine. We crossed the road and knocked on the front door of a lovely little cottage. Margaret let us in and we introduced ourselves. Margaret said, "I'll get you some hot food whilst you clean yourselves up a bit. There's plenty of hot water so you can have a good soak in the bath to warm up your bones. You look frozen. You're in the second room on the left with the bathroom opposite so I'll leave you to get on with it."

James said, "Go on with you pal you go first while I warm my backside by that fire. Just give me a shout when bath's ready."

Oh what luxury, I could have stayed in that bath for hours. I could feel the heat soaking into my bones. When I had finished I wiped away the tidemark and refilled the bath before calling James.

As soon as I was dressed I went down stairs into the living room by the fire. Margaret came in with a huge bowl of steaming hot homemade soup saying, "Get that inside you it'll warm the cockles of your heart young man. Then I'll fill you up with some roast beef and Yorkshire pudding to follow it."

And fill us up she did. Oh what a treasure. Just before retiring we went over the road to check the level of the fire. It would be a catastrophe to come out at daybreak and find the fire had gone out nor did we want to crawl out of bed in the wee small hours because the safety valve was screaming out into the night sky. After a good night's sleep I snuck out in the dark to poke up the fire and add more coal.

Next morning I was enjoying a nice cuppa with our host when James came bustling down stairs in a bit of a panic. He had slept in a bit longer than he wanted to and was flapping a bit and asking why we hadn't called him, but he soon settled down when I reported that the engine was fine. He was still muttering on about me not bothering to call him so I said, "I thought you needed lots of beauty sleep but it looks like it didn't work real good and anyway you would only 'ave gotten in my way out there."

Our host had a bowl full of steaming hot porridge that had been simmering on the slow combustion stove all night and she was trying to serve it up whilst having a good laugh at my comments about James. We only had to add lashings of golden syrup to start our meal. Fried eggs bacon and sausages were already sizzling on the stove and a heap of toast and boiling hot tea completed the meal.

Margaret followed us out into another cold dawn when we were ready to leave. She was carrying her trusty Kodak brownie camera to record our departure. The tanks were full of water thanks to a nearby hosepipe so James paid the bill, we said our goodbyes and we were away. I steered us out on to the empty main road (A62) and pointed her nose at that awful incline. The old tractor lifted up her head and away we went. James reckoned that we would travel in low gear because of the steepness and for safety. Changing gear on a steep slope is almost impossible so it was safer in the lower gear and up we went. It was a long way to Oldham and we knew there would be no streams or becks going up the hill so we had some concerns about water. Going uphill needed much more power of course and that meant much more steam. Steam is only very hot water so we expected to double our usage of that precious commodity. We had been told that there was a large pub close to the summit where we could get water. I soon noticed that there were a series of large stone troughs set into the banks of the road with mountain springs trickling into them. Apparently they had been placed there to give the cart horses a drink in the olden days. These would have helped in an emergency but parking would have been a huge drama so we intended to rely on the drums on the trailer. Checking the water level in the boiler was our biggest worry so we kept the level right at the top of the gauge and left the pump running to keep it there. We were attracting a vast amount of interest even that early in the morning with some cars actually following us up the hill. Probably hoping to see us come to grief.

When the pub came into sight we were a bit worried about water so I jumped down leaving

James to steer then I climbed onto the trailer and started the siphon. It was a bit dodgy balancing on the drawbar with the hosepipe but once it was running I could relax on the cart. I transferred the water from both drums before climbing back aboard.

It was just after 10 o'clock when we steered into the pub yard. The yardman was sweeping up around the buildings when I went over to ask if he had a hosepipe around somewhere so that I could fill the tanks. It only took a minute or two to drag one from his shed and he helped me to fill the bunker tank and both drums.

Meanwhile James was busy with his favourite occupations. He was telling everyone about our journey and obtaining vital nourishment as well a suitable liquid to wash it down and digest it. Pork pies were the order of the day and a nice drop of bitter was needed to wash it down.(Only shandy in my case).

Unbeknown to us the local grapevine was at work and as we were preparing to pull out onto the road a large lorry turned in and parked along side of us. A smart looking gent jumped out and called to us, "Are you the fellows from

Stavely, where ever that is? Are you on your way to Manchester University for Rag Week?"

James shouted in reply, "Aye that's right we are that pal. What's it got to do with you chaps then?"

"We're from the BBC television outside broadcast unit. We heard all about your trip and the boss reckoned that it would make a great story for the news tonight or tomorrow night. We'd like to film you travelling over the top of the Pennines if that's ok."

"Right you are then so long as you don't hold us up too much 'cause we still have a long way to go." James answered.

"We wont hold you up for long, All we need is a bit of back ground and your names, the rest we can do on the move." The gent answered.

We soon realised that the charity event was about to get some free advertising so everyone would be happy.

James opened up the steam valve with the tractor in high gear and away we went flat out at 12 mph. On this side of the hills the slopes were undulating which made it easy to keep a check on the water level and we enjoyed the drive except for a few light showers but as we were approaching Oldham we began to worry about our route. We had no idea where we were going or how to get to Manchester. With the cart on behind we had to more-or-less get it right first time. I had nightmares about trying to do a u-turn in the middle of either of these strange cities.

We just followed the A62 into Oldham then followed the signs for Manchester. On the outside of Oldham I was negotiating my way through some heavy traffic when a man stepped off the kerb and walked out into the street waving his hands like mad. Thinking the man was just another photographer or something James swore loudly trying to get the man to move away before I ran over him. I hadn't room to steer around him so James had no option but to stop.

"What the bloody hell are you doing you daft bugger," He yelled. "We damned near ran over you. Get off the bloody road." Undaunted the man approached and asked us, "Are you the lads from Yorkshire? Are you off to Manchester for the Rag week parade."

"Aye, yes that's right enough." James replied. "Who the hell are you then?"

"You lads is billeted wiv me for the night. If you follow me I'll take you to our Yard. It's just down street a bit and around t'corner. With that he set off along the street at a good pace so we followed behind. We ran alongside a very high brick wall for a distance then he turned down a side street on our left. Just a short way along the side street he waved us through some large wrought iron gates into a very big concrete yard. We pulled up in front of a massive brick building alongside another tractor. The tractor was an agricultural tractor like ours but it was a plain Jane in comparison. Pride of the Road was a bit of a show pony but the Fowler was very plain in black livery with very little brass fittings.

We were perving over the Fowler but our host, Malcolm, dragged us away. He had something better to show us. The huge brick building was in fact a very big cotton mill that Mal's family had owned and ran for generations. However it was now idle because it was far too antiquated to keep up to modern mills.

Under the main floor there were three huge Lancashire boilers. Apparently each one had been fired by two firemen, one at each side of the fire door. There was a heap of crushed coal in the yard. Mal estimated that there was probably 100 tons of the stuff stacked against the wall. The boilers ran 24 hours per day 7 days per week to feed an enormous steam engine that was used to power the mill. I regret that we didn't have a camera with us to record all this for posterity. The engine ran up through several floors of the mill right up to the roof. The main shaft was about 2 feet in diameter and it disappeared through a hole in the brick wall. At the other side of the wall was a huge room running the whole length of the mill and up to it's full height. This room housed only the flywheel and an outrigger bearing to support the flywheel and crankshaft. The wheel was about 25 feet in diameter and had 69, 2 inch diameter rope grooves across the face. A two inch spun cotton rope ran in each of the grooves like a vee belt to drive a separate shaft running through each room of the mill. Apparently the mill used to spin all the coarse waste cotton together to construct these massive ropes

We were simply stunned speechless until Mal called us back out to the engine. He had put in most of the day firing one of the boilers prior to collecting us. He proceeded to let steam run through the cylinders to preheat them for a while. Once they were up to temperature he opened up the valves to stir that great brute into life. We watched enthralled, as silently, it ran up to speed then eventually slowed down again as it used up the steam in the boiler. We realised that we were probably watching the final firing and running of that magnificent engine prior to the scrap men smashing her to pieces. Mal was very emotional probably holding back a flood of tears at the impending death of this beautiful piece of British engineering.

"Come on you two, show me your magnificent engine then we'll go get some fish and chips for our tea. Mal was rapt. Pride of the Road was beautiful and put his fowler to shame but he was satisfied with the performance of the fowler and he was looking forward to tomorrow. This was to be his first big outing since the major refit of the engine. Mal kept walking around our rig whilst we polished and preened her before damping the fire and checking her over.

Mal led us down the street to the best fish shop in town (his description not our's) where we stocked up with a heap of food. A quick call at one of the local pubs set us up for the evening even though it was "that Lancashire ale". One of the problems of travelling to foreign climes is that you often have to tolerate the local brew.

Mal lived a rough bachelor existence sharing a desolate decrepit terrace house with his father and brother. They appeared to be a wild bunch of renegades with fiery tempers and handy fists. After eating our impromptu meal the younger brother headed off for a romantic evening with his girl friend. The beds were rough the sheets dubious but we were stuffed. Once our guts were attended to all we wanted to do was sleep. This we did; and soundly until too about 2 am. at which time we were awakened by loud voices and savage swearing. We went down stairs to see what was happening and received one hell of a shock. Rod, the younger brother was a mess. His face was smashed to a pulp and was hardly recognisable. He could hardly stand let alone walk. He managed to tell us that a rival gang had roughed up his girl at a club they were attending so Rod cut loose in her defence. The father and Mal left us to clean Rod up as best we could, and they went out and collected their two other brothers from their homes nearby. They all went of together to see the local police who had wiped their hands of the whole affair. They said that the two groups had been at loggerheads for a long time and this was bound to happen one day. They refused once again to arrest any of the gang or take any action at all. Mal and co had a different view of the affray. They told the cops that if the gang were not behind bars by 6 am they would be exterminated. The family were prepared to take this fight to the limits. They knew where the gang lived and were going to sit on the doorstep until 6 am then take retribution. The police finally decided that the affair had gone much to far. They went out and arrested and charged all the gang members and locked them up in the cells for their own protection.

Whilst all this excitement was going on James and I walked around to the yard. We checked both tractors and stoked up the fires ready for and early start. Thank goodness Mal wasn't too involved with the family feud because we needed him to lead us into and through Manchester. Without him we may never have found the university at all. The rest of the night was a bit if a blur and we didn't get any more sleep

We eventually decided to cook up some grub

and a bucket full of tea to wash it all down before heading off out to the yard again. We vented our fury and frustration on the two tractors and the cart until they shone like new. As soon as it was light enough to be safe Mal hopped on board his engine slipped it into gear and with a few loud blasts of the whistle he was away. We settled in behind him and headed for town. Although it was still very early there was plenty of traffic to stare in wonder at our procession. The drivers hooted and tooted to us and waved madly as we wended our merry way into the city centre. Mal led us right into the chemistry department forecourt then left us to our fate whilst he went over to the arts section. His cart was already there and partly decorated. The very relieved float committee met us in the yard and helped to uncouple the cart and push it into a large archway out of any impending weather. We had a good chat then told them about the BBC television crew filming us travelling over the "TOP". They were hoping to be on the news in the evening to get maximum support for the rally. One of the students offered to take us on a guided tour of the city which we gladly accepted. Firstly we went to the Antrim hotel where a room had been reserved for us. We carried our luggage up to our room then cleaned ourselves up and changed into respectable clothes for the tour. I was only 15 years old and although I had been to York city shopping I had never seen anything like Manchester. I was quite amazed at some of the buildings but I didn't like the city at all in fact I hated everything about it. The noise, the filth, the hustle and bustle, pushing, and shoving were all alien to my nature. I was relieved to get back to our hotel and catch up with some sleep. James walked to the university yard a couple of times to check the engine. Initially we were going to drop the fire for the day but decided to keep a small fire in the box ready for an early start next day.

In the early evening I went with James to check the tractor and the fire. We went into the archway to see how the float was going. The tableau had been assembled on board and a group of students were working hard to decorate it. It was so hard to recognise that our cart was hidden beneath all that decoration and finery, Wow!!! What a show this was going to be and this was only one of the many floats that would make up the parade tomorrow.

When we arrived back at the hotel it was approaching time for dinner so James ordered a pint of best bitter for himself and a shandy for me then we made our way to the dinning room. We sat down at our table to enjoy the drinks whilst waiting for our first course when a familiar voice called out loudly, "There they are. I reckoned they'd be sitting in a pub somewhere boozing their heads off. I've caught them red handed this time so they can't deny it"

The voice belonged to Pat, James wife. James replied "Where the heck 'ave you come from and 'ow did you get 'ere. Hey where are the kids."

Pat of course had all the answers and said. "Oh Mam has a quiet week ahead and was bored stiff so she came over and took charge whilst I set off over here. Allan said the old van would make it all right. He checked the oil and water so 'ere I am and I'm starving."

"Right you are then, sit your arse down 'ere an' I'll get a drink for you." James said. "T'dinner'll be 'ere in a minute so I'll tell 'em there's another one to feed."

As we were finishing our meal the receptionist came over to our table to let us know that they had no more spare rooms so they wouldn't be able to fit Pat in anywhere. James decided that the huge bed in our room was big enough for three so we would be ok.

We took Pat's bags up to our room and James suggested we go for a tour of the central city areas before settling in for the night. We spent a couple of happy hours wandering about in the evening air. Pat was a city girl. Her family came from a very seedy area in Leeds city so she was very much at home here, whereas James and I disliked the place intently.

As we walked around the town I noticed small groups of women dressed to the nines with heavily made up faces and gaudy clothing standing around on street corners and shop doorways. From time to time they approached groups of men and slow moving cars. Being young and very naïve I had no idea what was going on but Pat and James seemed to be sharing some sort of jokes about it. James went over to chat with some of the women but the women didn't seem to like what he said as they shook their heads whilst looking across in our direction. It was many years later that I realised what had occurred. We had a common saying around North Yorkshire which went something like, "If you've never been to Manchester you've never lived." I could never understand what could possibly happen in Manchester that apparently didn't happen in our own cities in Yorkshire but of course it '<u>was</u>' all happening on our side of the Pennines just as it was on the Lancashire side. Today, when I look back on that evening in Manchester and throw in some of James character traits as well (I told you earlier that he was a wild, unpredictable sort of a guy) I am quite sure that he and Pat were trying to get one of the street ladies to deflower me whilst we were over there. However, it appeared that none of the ladies was prepared to take the risk because of my age. Thank goodness that nothing untoward actually happened. Even to this day I cannot see sense nor logic in paying a professional tart to enlighten a young man into the delights of sex at an early age or ever for that matter. The whole scene was so sordid and add to that the risk of nasty diseases which could scar a man for life. Maybe I've been fortunate that I have never needed to pay for sex: heaven forbid, and I never will.

So there we were and a full on day awaiting us for tomorrow. When we arrived back at the hotel I was headed straight for bed whilst the others decided to visit the bar for a nightcap or two. I was a little surprised at the amount of Lancashire ale James was consuming considering all the caustic comments about the quality or lack of it, the taste and even the texture of the stuff. Still I suppose James had really no choice; after all it was either foreign beer or no beer at all until we headed off home and as they often say "Any port in a storm." I did manage to get some sleep however before I felt James's cold feet in my back and Pat crawled in beside him.

I jumped out of bed early on Tuesday morning, quickly dressed and set out in the cold light of dawn to check the engine and attend to the fire. By the time I arrived back at the hotel James and Pat were ready to tackle the huge breakfast menu so I joined them eagerly. We had no idea when we might get lunch so it was important for me to fill to excess just in case.

"So you've finally got out of bed then," I asked "It looks as though we might have a sunny day even though it's going to be very cold at first. I've stoked up the fire and the engines ready to go, just a quick run around with the oilcan. The float appears to be finished but all the students were still in bed."

"Right you are then as soon as we get some of this grub tucked away we'll be off. Are you all set for a heavy day then pal?" James asked.

"As well as I can be." I replied. "This is a strange town and the streets will be chock-a-block with people. They'll be milling all around the tractor and it will be a nightmare trying not to run over any of them. With virtually no brakes to stop in a hurry and the cart on the back it'll be a miracle if we don't manage to mow a few of them down before day's end."

Pat chipped in and said, "Well I'm jolly glad you're here to steer for us Brian I don't think I could cope with it at all. I heard in the bar last night that "Pride of the Road" will be leading the parade. Is that true?"

"No-one has actually said so to me but last night when I shut the fire down some of the students were nattering near the float and they reckoned that it had to look extra special because it was to be the leading exhibit." I commented. "If we have to lead the parade they'll have to have someone walking in front of us to show us where to go and clear the way."

As soon as we had eaten we set off for the university yard. Some of the students were waiting for us to reverse around to the cart and hook it onto the draw bar. Once securely hitched up I straightened the steering and we pulled forward ready for the off. Two students appeared carrying a large rolled up banner, they were actually leading the retinue and I pulled in behind them. The parade was to assemble in a large plaza in the city centre so away we went. Some of the other exhibits were already in place and we were directed to our place at the head with our friend Mal tucked in behind on the resplendent Fowler. Mal had obviously spent many hours hard work on the Fowler since we last saw it. It still wasn't a "Marshall" but it looked very smart. We hopped down and spent some time chatting to Mal and admiring each other's engines whilst the rest of the parade was sorted out. Then the students reappeared with the banner unfurled and away we went with our steam whistles squealing.

As we turned into the main street we were

met by thousands of people. The footpaths were jammed tight with eager bodies even spilling out onto the roadway and the fun began immediately. The onlookers began tossing handfuls of coins and notes at us. There were hundreds of students surrounding us to collect the offerings and pack them into collection boxes. As soon as the boxes were full they were relayed to the back of the procession where they were stacked into a fleet of red vans kindly donated by Brooke Bonds tea company. The vans were soon filled up and they wheeled away to a central counting house to unload before returning to the fray. People were tossing donations down on us from multi-story buildings, shops, offices and houses as well as from the pavements and roadways. The scene looked like total pandemonium for hours as we wended our way round the city. The students carrying the banner changed places frequently as they tired and we just followed behind. Driving was a nightmare as we stopped and started ducked and dodged among the surging crowds. The noise was horrendous made worse by the steam whistles blaring out as well. Some of the coins landed on the tarmac surface of the road and were firmly embedded into the surface by the iron wheels. It didn't take long for people to realise that a strong kitchen knife or a screwdriver would retrieve the coin. When I cleaned out the smoke box at the base of the chimney next morning there were no less than 16 coins in there that had dropped down the chimneystack. The procession was very slow moving and we had to stop time and time again to prevent accidents. We were oh so glad when it was over and we could retire to the yard to unload the cart. We need not have worried about lunch because traders and shopkeepers kept rushing out to meet us with pies, cakes, sandwiches, etc as we rolled along. Pat seemed to be having a ball moving around in the crowd helping to collect the money off the road and pack it away. She was in her element, this was her sort of mob. James and I had discussed the possibility that we might be able to escape town and get as far as Mal's yard in Oldham before nightfall but that was never going to happen. The students rallied round us once the engine was shut down and we were wined and dined and entertained long into the night. James even had to consume large quantities of that foreign beer to appease our hosts. I have no idea what time I crawled into bed after a quick bath but it was very late and the rest of our mob were still hard at it.

I was settling down to an exhausted sleep when "Pat" slipped in besides me and cuddled up to my back. Next I felt her arm slide around my waist and feel about for the opening in the front of my pyjamas. The sensation was very pleasing as her fingers found what she was looking for. I was terrified. I wasn't able to move. I just held my breath and let it happen. I was pulled over towards her then on top of her. I wasn't exactly sure what went on but I can't deny that it was all very nice as we rolled around in that great big bed. When it was all over I was somewhat disconcerted not by the act but by who it was with. My partner in crime slid out of bed and whispered goodnight in an accent that was distinctly Lancashire rather than Broad Yorkshire. I was puzzling over this as the lady slipped out through the bedroom door and I admired her long flowing hair following her out into the dim light of the corridor. Hey! Bugger me! Pat had short permed hair that didn't even reach her shoulders. Who the hell had been in my bed with me, and doing all those nice things? I eventually fell asleep and heard no more until it was time to check the tractor and fire in the early morning. When I appeared in the dinning room James and Pat were already eating a big fried breakfast and as I joined them James gave me a big sly grin and said, "Now then young man, did you sleep well after all the excitement or were you past sleeping?"

I was looking down at my breakfast when I replied. "Heck, James you should know me by now. Once I switch off that's the end of it until morning. We 'ave a big day ahead of us if were to get out of this grubby town and out on to the moors. I didn't hear you and Pat come to bed. I hope you're sober enough and can stay awake long enough to get us back to good old Yorkshire today where at least you can wash all that foreign beer out of your belly with some quality Yorkshire ale. At least I won't 'ave to listen to you whinging about this other stuff."

I was sitting down at the table when I looked towards the kitchen hoping for more toast when the waitress walked out of the door with her long hair streaming out behind her. She brought the toast over smiled knowingly at me and said.

"Slept well did you pal. I hope your dreams

weren't too exciting. I bet you'll remember your first trip to Manchester for a long time to come."

"Yes thankyou," I replied "It's a good job one of us can get out of bed early or else we'd never get 'ome at all." Nothing more was ever said about my mysterious visitor but she definitely wasn't a ghost.

After another great breakfast we bade goodbye to our happy hosts and set off for Yorkshire. The road out of the city and through Oldham was a bit chaotic but eventually the traffic eased off so that we could roll along with gay abandon. Once we could see the outline of the Pennines looming ahead James was tempted to let the old girl go and we made very good time up to the pub at the summit in spite of water stops. It was always easier to locate water sources on the return trip due to some prior knowledge. After a quick lunch at the pub we rolled on down the hills at a cracking pace and slipped through Huddersfield with a minimum of trouble. We were getting quite adept at this lark now and were getting cheekier with the cops and other traffic. James decided that our run was good enough to reach the parking spot outside Leeds and hole up for the night. I was pretty knackered by the time I spotted the end of the street and Wesley ran out to meet us. We stopped and he jumped aboard for the short ride into the waste ground by his home. Wes helped James to shut down for the night because I was aching all over. Mrs Johnston came out to let me know that a hot bath was available so I left them to it and went for a long luxurious soak to warm up my bones and ease my aching muscles.

I don't know how she managed it but as soon as I was dressed Mrs Johnston placed a large bowl of delicious soup on the table in front of me. Soon we were all feeding our faces on home cooked food. James and I had to relate our story, to date, over and over again. Wesley wanted to know every little detail of our trip over the mountains as well as all that had happened in Manchester. Mrs Johnston was a little disappointed because we were a day early. Her husband was due to arrive home the next day and he was anxious to see the tractor and meet the two of us. After a good night's sleep I was up early to prepare for the road before a good breakfast to sustain us. I had been thinking about Wes and his passion for the tractor so I made a tentative suggestion at the table. Whilst Wes was out of the room I spoke to

James and Mrs Johnston saying, "If Wes's school is not too far out of our way and we have plenty of time anyway, why don't we give him a ride to school. He could put my old raincoat over his school clothes to keep them clean. His school pals will be thrilled as well?"

James replied, "Aye well now then that's an idea. As long as Mrs Johnson doesn't mind of course. He's been a great 'elp to us 'as Wes and he'd be right pleased I reckon."

"Right you are then that's all settled." Said Mrs Johnston, "As long as he behaves and keeps the coat on he'll love it. Thank you for thinking of him Brian. On your way along the road keep a look out for a BRS lorry with our George driving it. If he sees you in time he'll probable guess it's you and toot his horn at you."

So all was set. Wes was delirious. All his pals would see him driving the tractor, Wow!!!. This was going to be a great day for him. We timed our start to get to school about 8.30 am and away we went. There wasn't much room on the footplate so I had to stand on the step. As we approached the school yard I handed the steering wheel to Wes and sat on the coal bunker as he drove into

SHAKE RATTLE AND ROLL

the yard. Wes was like a dog with two tails. He didn't know which one to wag first. All the school crushed around us as Wes climbed down with a big grin from ear to ear. He was a natural show off and was loving the attention. Soon it was time for classes to begin and we still had a long day ahead of us so with many hoots and toots of the whistle we were off again. The road was busy but we had a good run through to Wetherby. There was a small stream running beneath the road just before we got to the A1 highway so we pulled onto the grass verge to fill up. As I was recoiling the hose after filling the bunker a big lorry rounded the corner and pulled up just along the road a bit. The driver jumped out and walked back to us. "Now then you lads, are you the fellows as went to Manchester last week?"

"Aye we are that," James answered "And I bet you're George Johnston from Leeds. We just gave Wes a lift to school on t'engine. He was right chuffed an all. The whole school, teachers and all, came over to 'ave a look."

"By heck that 'ud make 'is day then. Thanks for that. You must 'ave stayed at our place last night then."

"Aye we did that and right welcome it was an all. We owe you a great deal for your hospitality but t'wife wouldn't take owt from us so we spoilt young Wes instead."

"Aye well that's best road to settle matter and thanks again. I'd better get cracking so I'll say so long and 'ave a good trip home. See you later and thanks again."

Nearly everyone we met as we travelled around the countryside was really smashing to us and gave us the encouragement to do it all again. We had a pleasant run home then the usual shut down procedure and clean up before getting ready to face the music at school the next day.

Most of my classmates were in awe of me and envious of my trip however the teachers and head master were not amused at all. I was summoned to the study for a severe bollocking from the head master to account for my sins. Of course he had seen the television newsreel showing our passing over the Pennines and wanted an explanation. I knew that I was in real trouble but there was no point in denying it. He demanded that I justify taking absence from school and frittering my life away. The only excuse I could possibly have was that it was all for my education. After all I was 15 and that meant that school was no longer compulsory anyway. I apologised for my absence by saying, "Please sir, I am very sorry for my absence but I gave the matter a lot of thought before setting out. I realised that if I spend this year and the next three years studying very hard I may be lucky and get a chance to go to university. However, I was offered the chance to attend the university in Manchester and help to raise many thousands of pounds for charity at the same time. All I needed to do was work like mad and give up some of my weekend's of pleasures, tolerate a savage snowstorm and skip a few days school. I realise that I have no real excuse for my absence and I can assure you that I will work extra hard for the rest of term to catch up and atone for my neglect."

The Head replied, "That's all well and good and I agree with you that you have probably gained from the experience however I cannot have my students missing classes at will so I have no option but to punish you to set an example to the rest of school. You will write down the full story of your trip and bring it to me next week. I expect at least 4 full pages of script from you. Apart from that it must surely have been very enlightening to you and something you will remember for a long time."

"Yes Sir that's quite true. I have never been out of Yorkshire before. I have seen views of the mountains from the high Yorkshire dales but never been over the top of the Pennine Ranges. Manchester is amazing especially for a country boy like me and the chemistry department of the university astounded me. The architecture and buildings generally were a complete surprise but also the difference in the people and the social structure of the city, their way of doing things that's so different from around here were mesmerising"

"You amaze me O'Donnell. You sound like you have been living over there in Lancashire for many months not just a few days. Well done, you obviously took the time to study and learn as you travelled around the country.

The punishment was no task at all because I had already recorded most of it in writing anyway and the page number here will show that I have written many more that the designated 4 pages.

Chapter 4

HEADING NORTH BY NORTHWEST

As usual James and I were looking forward to the coming summer season to enable us to continue our epic travels around the north of England on our favourite steam tractor "PRIDE OF THE ROAD." A number of small repairs had been carried out over the colder months and the old girl was now in pristine condition ready for plenty of hard work. We began another season with a trip to Pickering for their annual steam rally which was becoming a large event these days with the inclusion of other forms of transport, such as vintage, lorries, cars, and motor cycles. Old fairground rides and fairground organs were now adding to the magnificent spectacle along with private collections of historic memorabilia.

I have covered our epic journey to Pickering in

earlier chapters so I intend to press on into new pastures. James called me to his home for a "conference of war" to work out a possible itinerary for coming months. Instead of returning home after our second visit to the rally at Pickering we decided to head much further north into county Durham. There was to be a rally and steam show at Chester-le-Street, which lies a few miles north of Durham city. The show ground was alongside the A1 highway thus giving us easy access. After a thorough study of our maps James decided that we needed to take a short cut across the north Yorkshire moors to shorten our journey and, hopefully reduce the traffic hazards. The route would contain a lot more hills, some of them quite steep, but the marvellous scenery would surely compensate for the hills and we were quite adept at negotiating steep hills by now. After all, only one year ago we had conquered the two steepest hills on any main road in England. Had we been starting from home we would have joined the A1 highway near Boroughbridge and stayed on it all the way. However, as we were some 40 miles or so east of the highway at Pickering it was decided that we would turn off at Helmsley on the way home and head north across the moors and through the Cleveland hills to Stokesley and Stockton-on-Tees from where there was a good system of roads straight to Durham city through Sedgefield. Going this way saved us the trauma of descending Sutton bank as we had done last year and there were far less towns to negotiate and only a couple of cities to cross.

Pat, James wife, had seen an advertisement for entrants in a competition at Whitley bay where the RAF Association were to hold a gala weekend. They were looking for a figurehead. Someone who could be crowned "Queen of Steam" for the weekend. Pat was a fair bit younger than James with a good figure and moderately good looks so she submitted a suitable photograph of herself wearing clean white coveralls to the committee for consideration in the event. In those days not many members of the fair sex, were prepared to get covered in oil and soot during a weekend jaunt on a noisy old tractor, and in fact Pat left most of the driving to me. The committee decided that Pat was the best entry, and all dressed up in white coveralls and looking the part she was given the honour.

We were to go on to Whitley Bay after the rally at Chester-le-Street. Whitley Bay was more than 100 miles from home so this was going to be our longest trip ever.

Once the Pickering rally was over we parked the tractor at the same farm that we had used the previous year and once again we were made so welcome. James had collected me whilst it was still dark on the Saturday morning and we hoped to arrive at the farm around daybreak. As soon as we arrived at the farm we got stuck into preparing for the road. By now we had gone through this routine so many times that it was only a matter of minutes before I had a steady curl of smoke climbing out of the chimney top. When our hosts called us in for a typical farmhouse breakfast the fire was burning well and most of the other work was in hand. We gave our hosts a hand with their chores around the farm whilst the fire did its job. It was around 9 o clock by the time we had enough steam to run the engine and that seemed to be a good time for a quick cuppa and some freshly baked scones before pulling out onto the moorland road heading to Kirbymoorside where we topped up the water tanks and headed for

Helmsley town about 6 miles away.

We turned north at Helmsley onto unknown territory. Neither of us had ever been along the road to Stokesley but it was a B class road running across the moor top and along the length of Bilsdale, a total journey of about 20 miles or so with an abundance of steep hills and descents. There was a suitable stream outside town so we topped up the water tanks and onto the B1257. I wish this story was about scenery and beautiful vistas because I could fill a whole book describing the views along the next 20 miles. We passed the ruins of Reivaulx Abbey on our left not far out of the town. These magnificent ruins stand up high above the surrounding landscape and can be seen for many miles. Shame on king Henry the eighth for ordering the destruction of this magnificent abbey just because he had a shit on with the Pope. At school we were taught to revere and respect our British royalty but how could we possibly do that when we have seen this savage vandalism. We complain today when so called artists disfigure our great architectural splendour but heck, a bit of paint is as nothing to what we were seeing here.

From here onwards there was little else except miles and miles of that magnificent spectacle, now known as the North York Moors, which flow on towards the mighty Cheviot hills now visible up ahead. Not far from an area known as Fangdale Beck we stopped for lunch and our usual maintenance work as well as more water. There seemed to be plenty of streams and becks up here on the moors relieving us of that worry as neither of us had ever been through this area of moors and mountains. We had learned our lessons on Sutton bank the previous year and now we looked for and found small local tracks leading off the roadway and onto the moorland. These provided fairly level parking places so that the water levels could be checked frequently to prevent damage to the boiler. Sometimes we were able to park near streams so that we could top up the tanks at the same time. Hindsight is a wonderful tool even back in the days of steam and even today is often quite handy. On the road once more with the sun on our backs we were soon rolling into Chop Gate at the far end of Bilsdale. Up here on the moor tops there was hardly any traffic so we were able to keep up a cracking pace. There were few villages or settlements to worry about and we were through Seave Green and heading for Great Broughton in double quick time. From here we could see Roseberry Topping about 5 miles to our right Roseberry Topping rises very steeply up off the moors and is without doubt the highest peak in the area.

We had been enjoying all this countrified driving but we were once again nearing civilisation. Stokesley was not far away. Stokesley is quite a large vibrant town situated at the junction of the A172 where it meets the A171 and A173 near the town centre. We needed to take the A171 for a short distance before turning off onto the B1365 which should take us to Middlesborough. This meant that we had to find a camping spot soon out of Stokesley as the day was fast closing in on us. We reckoned that we might find a suitable farmyard before we hit the outskirts of Middlesborough. Hopefully if we had a good day on the morrow we should be able to get to the area around Sedgefield but we had to find our way right across Middlesborough and Stockton-on-Tees first. Fortunately it was Sunday so an early start might serve us well.

It was becoming quite late as we passed through Nunthorpe village and continued towards the village of Hemington. There was a lovely country pub alongside the village green with a beck alongside. As there was plenty of room to park James declared his urgent need for a quick pint of Cameron's best ale before continuing on our way.

James said to me, "I'll just pop in 'ere to get a pint and check out the route a bit pal. You can oil her up and top up the water from this stream and I'll be back in a minute." Before I could remind him how late it was he jumped down and headed for the bar room door. "Thank you very much James," I thought. Just you look after yourself and don't worry about me. I was coiling up the suction hose when James re-emerged carrying a bag of Smiths potato crisps and a bottle of pop (cool drink) for me.

"Hey", he called out, 'Guess what? There's a big yard out the back of the pub and the landlord reckons that we can park the tractor there for the night. We'll leave it out here as long as we can because it's attracting a lot of interest and should help his trade a fair bit. The landlady reckons they have a couple of spare rooms they will let us have for the night and they'll provide us with a good bath and plenty of grub as well. The landlady is preparing a feed for us right now so look sharp about it. What do you reckon about your old mate now? Do I look after us or not eh?"

"Oh yea, smarty pants, that was a stroke of good luck not good management on your part." I said. James handed over my snacks then disappeared back into the pub to continue tasting the beer. After transferring some coal from the van to the coal bunker I unhitched the van and drove it around the back of the inn to make manoeuvring the tractor easier. I shifted the tractor away from the edge of the brook and parked it just off the roadway right in front of the pub sounding a few blasts on the whistle as I did so. I needed to leave the engine turning slowly over in neutral whilst topping up the boiler with the pump. Because the big open flywheel attracts a lot of attention when it is rotating slowly I left it running even when the boiler was full. There was still plenty of steam available as the fire settled down and by then all the kids for miles around seemed to be clamouring around as I took turns in lifting some of the toddlers up for a closer look. It was a bit of a nightmare keeping the others safely away from the moving parts and hot metal. The message seemed to have gained momentum because the pub was full and overflowing as people drove in from around the district to have a look at our 'Pride of The Road'. James came back out to take a turn in looking out for the old girl whilst I went inside for a good clean up and a good solid feed of country grub.

When I went back outside James was shutting the tractor down ready for the night having just decided to leave it out there rather than move it into the back yard. There was ample room and with the pub being open til late security didn't seem to be a problem. The publican said that he couldn't remember ever being so busy even when there were tour buses calling in and he needed extra staff to get through. I ended up washing beer glasses for a couple of hours so they could keep up. Talk about doing the washing up to pay for our dinner: we ended up with a free nights accommodation as well plus an open invitation to come back anytime we liked. Our hosts were stunned by the reaction to our presence and their stocks ended up very low awaiting the next delivery from the brewery.

I awoke very early to a different scenario. It was pouring down with rain as I built up the fire and checked the tractor for the road. Let's hope the old adage, "rain before seven, fine before eleven", would work out for us today. I crawled back into bed hoping for the best. James eventually woke me up and he was in a real old panic. "What the 'ells going on pal are you going to sleep all day. Look at the time. The days 'alf gone already, and your still in bed. Get your arse out of there and see to the fire."

Half asleep still I replied "Yea that might be a good idea James. Just 'ave a look outside the window pal. It's raining cats and dogs out there."

"Oh bloody 'ell that's all we needed. That's as maybe pal, but hey! we still 'ave to get going if we are going to get near enough to Chester-Le-Street in reasonable time, rain or no rain. I bet yon fires about out or damn near it so look sharp while I go and see about some grub." James retorted.

"It's a pity you weren't awake a couple of 'ours ago then you might 'ave seen me get up and go outside to the tractor and attend to the fire," I spat out angrily. "If it 'ad been left to you it would 'ave been out by now for sure."

Dressing quickly I went straight down to the kitchen following the delicious smells of frying food. I left James to check the fire and water levels whilst I went into the kitchen for breakfast. Boy oh boy did our host put on a feast? She reckoned that we'd need to feed up big because of the inclement weather. The landlady had also packed up a great bag full of sandwiches and cakes to take with us. I was still wading my way through the mountain of fried food on my plate when James came in and informed us that he thought the rain was easing off and we might yet have a decent day for our travels. James's observations about the weather proved correct and by the time we were ready to hit the road we faced only steady drizzle. For once James copped the brunt of the weather because his position on the platform was besides the spinning flywheel so he was constantly sprayed even when the rain eased off a bit. James had little or no movement to drive the tractor whereas I was spinning the big steering wheel which kept my blood running and I was quite warm except for my hands. However, even though he was standing next to the fire box James was quite nithered (frozen) and complaining madly about the conditions.

We soon crossed the A174 as we headed for and skirted Middlesborough on the A1032 towards Stockton-on-Tees. Traffic wasn't a problem this early on a Sunday morning but once in the towns and suburbs water supplies were once again a problem. Often we spotted becks or streams but they were out of reach off our suction hose. Whenever we saw water we always topped up to the maximum so the bunker was generally full at all times so we could manage the odd awkward stretch without panicking. We crossed the A66 before finding our route onto the A177. In no time at all we were through Stockton-on-Tees and rolling along the A177 for Sedgefield. Out in the countryside again we could relax as there was plenty of water and very little traffic. Because we had consumed such a huge meal for breakfast we kept rolling along until we were only a few miles short of Sedgefield where we found a lovely secluded picnic spot with a suitable stream running through it. James declared that this was the ideal spot for a serious lunch stop, both for us and the tractor. I had the water filled up in no time at all then we settled down to a leisurely lunch.

The morning run had been idyllic inspite of the early rain and we were well ahead of schedule giving me time for a stroll along the pretty little stream whilst James settled in for a bit of a nap.

It seemed a pity to have to move on again but we had to get to Chester- Le-Street before we could really relax. Once clear of the town James decided to stay on the A177 which cut across country for a while heading for Cornforth and the dreaded A1 highway. Even though it was Sunday afternoon it was bound to be busy. We had seen very few lorries all day but the A1 would have lorries aplenty.

James spotted a small stream just before we came to the Great North Road and we topped up the tanks. Just getting back onto the road with such a slow moving vehicle was a nightmare and in the end James lost his temper, opened the steam valve and charged onto the highway with gay abandon. The steam whistle let out a long shrill scream as I pulled on the chain and blended in with the squealing of brakes and loud hooting of horns all around us we charged off again. The tractor was never in any danger of collision although some of the cars had very near misses. Today we complain about road rage as though it was a modern phenomenon but you should have heard all the dialogue that day. We heard lots of new swear words and we were called everything other than the 'gentlemen' that everyone knew we were. After all we had paid our road tax just as they had. There's nothing like 10 ton of scrap metal rushing towards you belching forth clouds of steam and smoke to get instant clearway, even if a few rude gestures and swearwords are the ultimate reward. No one ever tried to run us off the road or force us to stop just to "have a go at us" as a result of our behaviour but we always tried to merge in with other traffic to prevent problems with the law. We were always aware that the rules, which allowed us to travel on modern roads, were written many years ago and if we caused too much disruption the authorities might revoke them and force us to use low loaders to transport our tractor around to the shows. I am glad we lived in an era that allowed us to have all this fun on the roads prior to motorways and dual carriageways.

At this point we were only a few miles short of Durham city and we had enough water to see us through the city and, hopefully there would be a suitable water point somewhere clear of the town streets but the city ran along the A1 for a fair distance beyond the city centre. We were about to enter the city proper when James spotted a fair sized beck, which was a tributary of the river Wear. There was a clear area on the bank so I topped up the tank and coal whilst James oiled up again. We always dreaded entering a city, especially one like this where we had no knowledge of streets and traffic problems. All we could do was plough our way into and through the main streets and hope for the best. Because the tractor was such a great novelty most people were ready to assist us to find our way through with a minimum of stress. We were to stay on the A1 all the way through to our destination so with full tanks it only remained for James to keep a good fire going and myself to steer a steady course out of the place. Our passage as it turned out was straightforward and we were soon clear of the town and searching for a suitable place to park the tractor for the next week. The old A1 actually slips past most of Durham city on the western side so a large part of the main town lay away to our right hand side. Our route took us through one or two small villages such as, Pity Me, and Plawsworth then as we approached our destination we spotted a small stream running close to the road.

"Hey James" I called out 'I'm going over there to the right and along that laneway so we can fill 'er up". The road was clear so I spun the steering wheel around and James pulled up on a bit of grass beside the road.

Having filled the tanks and oiled up we were just about to turn around and head off back to the main road when a farmer stopped his old Austin car alongside to inspect the tractor. During the ensuing conversation the farmer told us that he was involved with the rally and that there was a farmyard on the side road that goes to Hetton-Le-Hole. He told us where to turn off, then run up the hill until we could see a large concrete circle that looked a bit like a large water tank on our right hand side. This, it appeared, was a coalmine ventilation shaft and alongside it there was a large clear area where we could park up in safety. Both James and I were ever so glad to pull into the farmyard and drop the fire. We were both absolutely bone weary. After putting the old girl to rest we cleaned ourselves up, unhitched the van and headed into town to find a café before setting off back home to West Yorkshire.

The next weekend we had to leave early for the long drive up the A1 to Chester-le-street. This meant preparing all week so that on Friday night I could get stuck into my chores, sort out the pigs and poultry to minimise the work for Saturday. Off we went shortly after daybreak in the old Austin van for even in that it was a two hour journey or so. We soon had a fire going after checking the boiler and then we were able to boil some water for a welcome cup of tea. Whilst James was oiling up the tractor I toasted some thick slices of bread in the firebox then fried eggs, bacon and sausages on the coal shovel that was used to stoke the fire. I could never work out why our impromptu meals out on the road always turned out so delicious. Maybe it was a combination of the barbecue effect of cooking on the open fire and the picnic style meal sitting on the ground, or possibly the added flavour of coal dust from the shovel. The very special, newly baked bread from James's parents village bakery probably helped as well.

It was only a short drive to the show grounds where we were welcomed effusively by the committee members and congratulated for travelling such a long way to be there to help them make a fantastic day of it (which it certainly was).

That day I got my first look at a White Bros. Gavioli fairground organ. It was absolutely massive but still needing some more love and care to bring it up to scratch. It had a display of moving figures pretending to play the various instruments needed to make up a full orchestra as well as dancing ballerinas. The whole thing was controlled by a series of cardboard plates hinged together with lots of holes punched in them to open the valves. There were small monkeys playing the smaller drums as well as a very large monkey thumping out the beat on a huge drum. The volume was massive and someone told us that the local children were singing and dancing to the music in the town streets. The organ was situated right at the top of the field away from most of the activity to allow the music to flow out over the field without deafening anybody. A large compound fairground steam tractor was parked beside the organ to provide the necessary power to make it play and also to light up all the coloured lights around it. These large steam fairground locomotives were used to haul all the fairground machinery from town to town and then to provide electricity to drive the rides and light up the fairground as well. It has been said that some of the bigger locomotives pulled up to as many as 5 four-wheeled trailers full of equipment when the fairground moved to a fresh venue.

The day really was a huge success and we were convinced that it was well worth all the effort on our part to be part of it. We left the showground that evening with huge smiles on our faces and serious promises to return next year. That night we only had to go back up the hill to the yard where we had parked on the way in because the tractor was staying there for another week before heading off even further north to Whitley Bay to a carnival organised by the RAFA.

This next weekend was to be somewhat different to our normal routine because James's wife Pat was to be the star of the show and was coming with us all the way. We prepared everything during the week so that we could leave as soon as James was ready after a hard days work. I pitched in and organised the van ready for the trip. Whilst James was eating and preparing himself for the journey I removed surplus tools and pipe fittings from the van then put in our travelling kit, food and tent etc. ready for off. We had decided to drive to Chester-le-street in the evening so we could light the fire before setting up camp.

It was always a bit of a crush in the old van by the time it was stocked with sacks of coal as well as all our other needs. Sometimes it was possible to obtain coal on site but because we always travelled at the weekends it was sometimes a problem so we carried our own whenever possible. Also much domestic coal wasn't really suitable for the boiler so it was better to pre-order from our local supplier in the village. That way we could be sure to get decent hard if not always good steaming coal. After 60 miles or so huddled up in the van it was a great relief to climb out and stretch our legs. Although it was drizzling rain when we arrived it was all hands to the wheel. Pat was in charge of organising supper for us whilst I lit the boiler fire and James prepared the boiler and the tractor ready for an early start. The first part of our journey was along the dreaded Great North Road so the earlier we could get away the better and rain or not we had to do it. After about 15-16 miles we had to negotiate our way through the city of Newcastle cross the bridge over the river Tyne then head off towards the coast and eventually to Whitley Bay. We were becoming old hands at negotiating our way through traffic often using the term "Hey, we're bigger than you and a lot site uglier so let us through." Often all the noise, clouds of smoke, and belching steam was quite off-putting to the uninitiated and gained us right of way.

Once under way along the main road our next concern was a suitable supply of good water. We needed to find a supply very close to the outskirts and approaches to Newcastle to make sure that we could get all the way through the city without stopping to fill the tanks. Being still early in the day traffic was bearable all the way through to the bridge over the river Tyne then the tractor was quickly inundated with swarms of commuter traffic all trying to get a clear access onto the bridge and off again at the other side. James was just in the process of slowing down as we merged into a heavy stream of traffic moving onto the bridge when a car driver made a fatal error. He hesitated and created a space for the front wheels to enter. I shouted out to James swung the big steering wheel hard left and grabbed the chain that operated the steam whistle as James whipped open the steam valve to rev up the engine. Just for good measure James also flicked open the drain valves on the steam cylinder and began squirting jets of steam over the nearest cars. Much daunted and with horns blaring the cars allowed us onto the bridge and away. Negotiating our way through the traffic had used more water than expected and we were desperately searching for more when I spotted a large stone trough ahead. There was nowhere suitable to park but I squeezed in just beyond the trough jumped off and quickly threw the suction pipe into the water. By the time that following traffic realised that we were not actually penned in and could move on we had sucked up most of the water and took off again as the drivers practiced their horn blowing skill once more. In the past I had found out that sometimes it was necessary to grab some water in a hurry so I kept the hose ready for instant action.

Still on the A1 highway we cleared the city then as the houses began to thin out we spotted the signs for Whitley Bay and the coast. This meant a sharp right hand turn and it looked like everyone must be heading home for lunch. The traffic was very heavy for a short while then a large lorry approached the intersection and flashed his lights to give us the right-of-way, which was a great relief. From a standing start it takes a while to clear a big road junction like that and we waved merrily to the driver. We got the impression that he was tickled pink at seeing us and was very happy to let us go through first so he could get a better look at us. Shortly after the junction James spotted a small beck running close by so we happily filled up the tanks once more. From here it was about 4 hours drive to the coast with only a couple of major road intersections such as crossing the A19.

As we approached the out skirts of Whitley Bay I spotted a lone cyclist puffing along the road towards us. As he came near it became obvious that the man was in uniform and was in fact one of the local constabulary, a copper in fact. At first he appeared to not notice us but as he drew close he halted his progress and began to climb off his bike. He parked the bike besides the kerb and stepped out into the road. Then raising his right hand he tried to stop our progress. It was not unusual for us to face the long arm of the law because of my age about 15 years at that time and I was actually steering the tractor on a public road. This as it turned out was not the trouble today.

He shouted out loudly so as to be heard above the noise of the tractor, "Now then you lads, where the 'eck do you think you're ganning to." Although it must have been only too obvious that the only place we could be going to was Whitley Bay.

James shouted back, "Into town you daft old bugger. We're t'main part of't big show this weekend. We're leading the parade in the RAFA carnival and this lady, pointing to Pat is to be the Queen of Steam for the day."

"Aye well I've got some bad news for you lads. You see we 'ave a town bylaw that states that no iron tyred vehicles is allowed on the roads of this 'ere town so you'll 'ave to turn round and go back to where you've come from." Shouted the copper.

Unfortunately James could be very belligerent

when tormented and he had a vicious temper when he got his back up. He started to climb down from the platform with all his hackles up ready for a fight and started yelling back at the cop. I screwed the parking brake on and jumped down as well and I was trying to calm James down when a large Humber Super Snipe motorcar pulled up along side me. The driver got out and spoke to me saying, "Now then young man what's happening here. Is there some sort of a problem? You lads must be on your way to the RAFA carnival in town."

"Yes that's right". I answered. "This police man says that we aren't allowed to enter the town on iron wheels cause there's a bylaw that says it's not allowed."

The man went over to James and the copper and informed us that he was in fact the town mayor and the problem was easily sorted. He walked over to a nearby house and asked permission to use their telephone. This was granted and he went inside to make a number of phone calls. Having got things organised he came outside again carrying a tray on which there was a number of cups of tea.

Once we were all settled down and drinking our tea, all that was except the cop who steadfastly refused his as he was still bristling with indignation and still on duty. The Mayor said, "I've gotten it all sorted but it will take a few minutes for the others to arrive." In fact it was nearly half an hour before 'they' all arrived and the meeting could begin. He called the meeting to order and then conducted an impromptu council meeting right there and then on the road verge. One man proposed a motion that the old bylaw be repealed for one month each year to allow for the carnival. This was duly seconded then enacted into law. Everyone was satisfied except the hostile policeman who climbed back on his bike and rode off muttering obscenities along the way. James turned to me saying, "I reckon we had better watch our every move whilst we are here in town or yon old bugger will have us for sure."

I replied "I reckon you're right there James. I'll bet he can be a nasty piece of work when he sets his mind to it."

These early problems were easily sorted out and we settled down to a fantastic weekend of fun and frivolity. There were a good many steam vehicles as well as vintage cars. James proclaimed that the beer was excellent but he needed to try a few different brews whilst we were there just to make doubly sure. The first day ended up with a ball which lasted most of the night. The natives held us in high regard and we were looked after in true north country style.

We didn't get much sleep whilst we were in town but 'what the heck?' we had a ball. It was very difficult to crawl out of our tent the next morning and the fire had gone out so it was back to basics again. Eventually all good things come to an end and we had to think about our return trip home to Stavely. We had to face 100 miles or so mainly along the Great North Road not to mention a few big towns and cities as well.

James and I believed that we were masters of the art of bulldozing our way through heavy traffic until we slid to a standstill at a set of traffic lights in the middle of Newcastle on the way home. A car driver was too busy staring at our old tractor that he forgot to look where he was going and ploughed into a car in the middle of the intersection causing a massive pile up with us in the middle. The police duly arrived to try and sort out the mess but they were not getting along too good. A young policeman moved over the road to stand close to the tractor and have a good look and a bit of a chat whilst his superiors tried to sort out the mess. During the conversation I mentioned to the young policeman that I thought these northern coppers didn't seem to be anywhere as smart as the Lancaster Constabulary in Manchester. The young man retorted, "What the hell do you mean? What can they do that we can't?"

I gave him a cheeky grin and said, "We were involved in a similar incident on the outskirts of Manchester and the police there were smart enough to realise that all they needed to do was get this great monstrosity out of the way and let the rest sort themselves out. The copper scratched his head then walked across to his colleagues for a bit of a natter. The sergeant in charge came over to us and had a good look at the situation saying, "Do you lads reckon you could get through that gap and get that heap of scrap out of here?"

"Oh aye that we could an' all James replied, there's plenty of room for us. What do you think pal?" He asked me, "your driving after all."

"It'll be touch and go but I reckon I can squeeze though and maybe the cars will ease back a bit when they see us charging at them, I replied".

"Ok then lets have a go and see what happens," the sergeant added.

James grabbed the chain to blast the whistle so that everyone knew we were about to move into the fray and away we went slowly but surely. We had the cylinder cocks open to clear the condensate from the cold cylinder making a vivid display of steam which further assisted the car drivers to make a decision and let us though. The cars gave us enough room to squeeze through and away we went leaving the constabulary to clean up the mess.

The remainder of the return trip took us two weekends fortunately without any more incidents. Over the next couple of months we travelled to a number of agricultural shows and steam fairs before putting the old girl to sleep for the winter.

Chapter 5

A NEW BEGINNING

Early the following autumn as winter was beginning to settle in James Alderton called at our farm house one cold evening searching through the old, stone, farm buildings, calling out and frantically searching for me. He caught up with me in the poultry shed where I was collecting the daily egg harvest ready for cleaning, grading and packing.

"Now then young man he called out. I was beginning to think you'd gotten lost. Hurry up with that 'cause I need to talk to you.'

"Ok James I'm about done here and we can chat while I sort and pack this lot. If you go into the packing shed the fire is lit but it may need a few logs to brighten it up. Put the kettle on an' all then we can drink tea and talk.'

When I entered the packing shed James was

standing with his bum over the fire but the kettle was boiling ready for me to make tea.

'What the heck's up with you James?' I asked him. 'How come you're in such a tiss about some'at? Is your 'ouse on fire or what?'

'Nay it's nowt like that lad, it's about this letter 'ere'. James passed a letter to me so that I could understand what all the fuss was about. I quickly scanned the type written letter before handing it back to him and querying, "Where has all this come from, pal?"

"Aye well it came from an advert in't 'Worlds Fair' paper. A bloke I know over Northallerton way is looking for people to invest in a showman's engine. He 'as three rich pals who are ready to invest some money with him but they know nothing about steam tractors and they don't want to get their hands dirty either. They are townies see, used to a bit of office work and run posh businesses. My pal thought of me and asked me to come on board, but as you know Pride Of The Road takes up all my spare cash and keeps me poor as he well knows. Laurence, knowing all this, has suggested sharing the tractor five ways and my share will be doing the work and getting the old girl going. The rest of the group will buy the tractor and any material cost to get it ready for the road then we will be able to play with it. I just thought you might like to come along and get involved.'

"What sort of tractor is it and where and when can we see it?" I asked.

"Aye well that's t'first problem you see. It's parked in a boiler yard at Castleford. The fairground outfit what owned it parked it in the yard ready to have a new set of boiler tubes fitted in time for the next season. The elderly bloke what owns the yard said they could park it there whilst they decided whether to buy one of the new heavy diesel tractors instead of continuing with steam power. The yard owner said they would have to pay him 5 shillings per week parking fee whilst it was there. The owners have never paid him any parking fees so he advertised the engine for sale to recoup his money legally. If we want it we will have to pay the back rent. 25years at 5 shillings per week is a tidy sum of money but the engine is unique. You see Foden motor company only ever built 3 such engines and the other 2 have definitely been cut up for scrap metal. This ones t'last you see that's why we want it. If we buy it, it will need 42 new boiler tubes which would need fitting to the boiler plates before we do anything else so I need to go down to inspect the rest of it. I intend to go on Saturday if you are keen to see it."

"Hey! You bet, if Dad will let me off for the day that is. I can't wait to see her. What time will we be setting off."

"It will have to be very early 'cause it's about 60 miles away. Can you get away about 7 o'clock say."

"I should be ready by then. Mam will help me with the hens if I see to the pigs."

"Okay I'll see you about then but I think Pat will be coming so do you mind sitting in the back?"

"No I have some old cushions that I can bring. Do I need to bring any grub with we?"

"Aye well, I know how much you like your grub so we'll call in at Mam's as we go past and grab some cakes and pies and buns."

By Saturday morning I was ready to leave at 7am but James was late as usual. It was nearly half past when the old van pulled into our yard. I threw in the cushions that I had collected and we were away. A short stop at the baker's shop then full steam ahead. The old Austin was not the fastest vehicle around but it was reliable and fairly economical.

We had some trouble finding Hepworth's boiler yard but by the time the engine was ready to drive away we would be able to find it blindfold. The yard was in a back street and we were amazed at the size of it. James drove in through the big double gates and parked near where we could see a rusty old wreck of the tractor. It still had the overhead canopy in place so it was easy to see. James walked into a large shed with an office in front of it and called out. A very large, elderly man wearing badly soiled overalls waddled out through the double doors to meet him.

"Nah then, what brings you lads into my yard on a weekend?"

James explained that we were the guys from Stavely and were there to have a good look over the traction engine.

"Oh well that's ok then. I'm Frank Hepworth what owns this 'ere yard so you go and look over yon' engine but be careful you don't hurt yourselves in all that scrap metal. I'll be in the shed 'til dinner time so give me a shout if you want any help.

'James this engine is huge, I've never seen another engine so big', I said.

"Aye thou's right about that. There'll be a hell of a lot of scaping, painting and polishing afore we get her to a show ground somewhere."

Prospector is the name of this Foden Steam Fair ground Engine.

She is unique, the only one left in the whole world.

These types of locomotive were built exclusively for the travelling fair ground industry before the days of modern diesel lorries. They were built to transport the fairground rides and equipment from town to town then drive a built-in DC generator to power the rides and light up the fairground. I was told that at some times Prospector and other similar engines pulled up to five large trailers loaded with equipment and living vans

'It is very big as you say Brian. It is a twelve horse power twin cylinder compound steam engine mounted on the boiler. According to this old log book here she weighs 18 tons dry and about 24 tons with a full load of coal and water. The rear wheels are 8 feet 9 inches in diameter (2.7metres) with 4inch (10cm) solid rubber tyres on the outside. She is sprung on all wheels and has a three speed transmission. She is reputed to do 25mph in top gear if any one is game to steer her. The DC electric generator in front of the smoke stack will light up a small town or power a large fairground.

"Have you bought it yet or have you to decide after today's inspection?"

"It's stood here for a very long time and there will be all sorts of problems, some of which we won't be able to see but at first glance it doesn't look too bad so lets crawl all over and see what we see."

"Right pal I've opened the drain cocks on the cylinders so get a hold on that bloody great flywheel and we'll see if the motion is still working. It might be frozen solid. When I shout give it a great heave then we'll see. If it turns over freely we should have a deal."

Amazingly the wheel turned over relatively easily due to the fact that the overhead canopy was still weatherproof and the working parts had kept relatively dry. It appeared that a large amount of grease had been caked over the moving parts when she was laid up to help keep the weather at bay

After half an hour with the oil can and penetrene solvent we stopped for lunch. When we returned the motion turned over quite freely and there didn't seem to be any big problems to concern us.

Next and most importantly was the boiler inspection. Although we knew that the long smoke tubes were burned out the rest needed to be checked. Once it was re-tubed it would need to be pressure tested to make sure it was safe to fire up again. James opened up the fire door at the front whilst I mounted the driving plate to open up the firebox and ash pan. We were both surprised at how easily the various doors etc moved to open up the tubes. It appeared that they had always been lubricated with colloidal graphite when the engine was working.

I won't bother telling you about the clean up and refurbishment other than to say that everything was massive, far more so than Pride Of The Road ever was and it would take us many weekends of backbreaking toil before we could fire up the boiler to find out if our efforts were in vain or not. One problem that was obvious was that someone or other had remove the twisted brass tubes that fitted around the canopy supports. These tubes, although not a working part are essentially part of the engine presentation. She looked naked without them and they would have to be replaced sometime or other but there were firms in the business who would make them to order. Everything that we checked seemed to be in workable condition. We were still climbing over the engine when Frank called us into the office for a well earned cuppa tea.

"Well how did you go you lads? Have you come to any decisions about buying it? We are sick of it clogging up the yard and will be pleased to see the back of it."

James replied, "I'll be quite honest with you Frank, we would like to see her going again and provided the boiler tests out A1 we should be able to do a deal. The rent money is a bit of a problem so I don't suppose that you would negotiate on that score."

"Not a chance James it owes us and we need to get paid so that we can settle the legal problems of ownership. However having said that, me and my crew will give you all the help we can including the boiler work provided you get stuck in and help yourselves if you have a cheque with you now I will see that all the scrap is cleared up around it and I will order in the new tubes on Monday. I will expect a cheque for the tubes next time you come. Have you any experience and knowledge how to get the old tubes out and roll the new ones in."

"I am a qualified steam fitter, boilermaker and plumber but I have never tackled anything this big so I might have to lean on you chaps a bit." Replied James. I'll write you a cheque now including the new tubes if you know how much they will be then we'll get going. It's a long way to come each time but neither of us can do owt about that." Once the financial arrangements were complete and a quantity of tea consumed we said our goodbyes and headed home.

My mind was agog with information that would need interpolating in the future but I was thrilled to bits with the outcome of our trip. The next weekend was earmarked to make a start on the boiler. There was no point in working on anything else until we could be sure the boiler would pass a full test series. If we got it wrong and the boiler burst at full pressure most of the yard would be demolished and if anybody was in the yard they would be seriously hurt or worse still, killed.

After a very early start we arrived in Castleford as the sun came up then we were straight on the job of restoring Prospector. As I have stated the boiler tubes were our main concern so we removed the ash pan from the firebox and pulled it forward out of our way. Using a very large hammer we were able to loosen and remove the heavy cast-iron fire bars to gain access to the inside of the box and the ends of the tubes. Using a special drift to protect the end of the tube James attacked one of tubes using a very heavy sledge hammer with a short handle.

After quite a long time, with many harsh words and some swearing James crawled out from under the box and threw down the hammer.

"Buggered if I know, the damned things haven't budged. There must be a bit of a trick to it but it beats me how to get them moving. Somebody must have welded the buggers in place."

I passed James a fresh cup of tea, just before old Frank waddled over with a huge grin on his face ready with some advice.

Frank was carrying a specially heavy hammer and what looked like a special tool to fit deep into the ends of the tubes. I poured out another cuppa for him and we all settled down for a bit of a rest and chat.

"Now then you lads, It seems as though you need an expert to show you the way. When I have finished this tea I'll show you youngsters how it's done but don't even begin to think I'll do more than one or two then its up to you fellows to manage on your own."

Once Frank was ready, much to our amazement he rolled over and under the box then somehow sat up inside it. "Now then pass me that hammer and dolly then watch what I do. I know you can't see a lot in here because of my great big belly but you should see enough to know how to do it."

Frank placed the dolly firmly in the end of the tube picked up the hammer in his other hand then gave 3 or 4 tentative hits on the end of the dolly followed by one massive blow. He repeated this action 2 or 3 times and out popped the tube. The tubes are only rolled tight at each end so once they move about 2 inches they are free and can be pulled out all the way by hand. Frank knocked out two more tubes before rolling out saying "Well there you are now you know how, just get on with it. You can borrow the dolly and hammer till you get them all out."

Frank proceeded to straighten his cramped old

legs then waddled back to the workshop. James scrambled into the fire box with some difficulty and managed to loosen a few tubes. James's problem was that he was built the wrong way for boiler work. He was very tall with long gangly legs and nothing quite fitted into the right shape for the job. His head and shoulders were too high in the box which meant all the other parts were at the wrong angle especially for the lower tubes. He was practically standing on his head at times

When James rolled out I took over and had a go. James laughed saying, "Thou's nobbut a bit of a lad and no way near strong enough to start them tubes off. Just give me a minute to get me wind then I'll 'ave another go."

I soon found a comfortable position and popped one of the lower tubes out then followed that with a few more. It wasn't easy but I soon had all the lower tubes out before crawling out for a rest.

James remarked "Well bugger me you must be a lot stronger than you look lad."

"Nah," I replied, "I think it's just a knack and 'cause I am small enough to be comfortable."

"Aye well if it's like that you can crawl back in

the hole and I'll pull them out from the front."

It took surprisingly little time to remove the rest of the tubes and delegate them to the scrap metal dump nearby. The holes in the boiler plates then had to be thoroughly cleaned so that the new tubes would make a serious water seal when installed. Each pipe had then to be cleaned especially both ends, again to ensure a perfect water seal. One by one the pipes had then to be very carefully bumped into place in the boiler plates using a log of wood to protect the pipe then a special expanding roller tool was rotated inside the new pipe to expand it to become a very tight fit in the holes. If any of the pipes were a bit too loose they needed to be expanded before fitting to prevent them turning as the ends were swaged out to fit.

When all the pipes were in place we had to fill the boiler with water, seal off the outlets and attach a hand operated pressure pump to increase the pressure to one and one quarter times the working pressure (which was 100 psi). The pressure rose slowly until it neared 100 psi at which point one or two small leaks appeared around the new pipe ends and these were quickly sealed up with more rolling pressure inside the faulty joint. The boiler was left at that pressure over night then increased to 125psi the next morning. Hurray!!! This meant that the boiler was now sound and ready for use. That only left the pressure safety valve to be stripped cleaned and carefully reset to 100psi.

To minimise our travelling Frank offered us the use of an old stone cottage in the corner of the yard which had once been accommodation for the yard security guard but had long been disused. It was great for us to camp in, brew quantities of tea and cook bacon and eggs to go on Mrs Alderton's fantastic bread, thereby saving a lot of our time and costs as we could now stay in town over the weekend and work from first light until dark. Only my dad was not happy but I pleaded that I needed a holiday from farm work. Dad thought I might be leaving too much to my mother but we shared the pain. My sister Jean absolutely refused to help Mam out and Mam always said that it was easier to do it herself than try to get Jean to help

I really enjoyed the challenge of our first weekend working on Prospector unfortunately I had to forego many of the later events due to pressure of work at home and school work. At that time dad was working on contract for his boss and much of the time he worked miles from home. Most days he left for work before daylight and returned after dark leaving most of the work to me and mam.

Then one afternoon James came over to find me for a bit of a chat. The weekend prior to that day they were able to take Prospector for a short run around town. Pat acted as steersman but she was terrified of all that machinery so James came to ask me if I could get the next weekend free to drive the tractor home. As it turned out Dad was between contracts so he was able to let me go.

James drove the old van to Castleford where he and I with some assistance from Pat prepared the tractor for the road. We had to drive along some busy main roads as well as through a number of busy towns and cities. It was late morning before we pulled out of the boiler yard with much fanfare and whistles then onto the ring road and home with Pat keeping up a rear guard in case we needed help. Prospector had extra bunker tanks fitted in front of the firebox so water supply wasn't as critical as usual but still a concern. She had been designed and set up for long distance haulage. There was a main road from Castleford to the outskirts of Leeds then we were on familiar ground with the tractor running sweetly we travelled at about twelve miles per hour. Amazingly the machine was much easier to handle than Pride of the Road due to the springs and rubber tyres also it was much easier to steer at speed than crawling on iron wheels. Stopping was still a problem with no running brakes but the extra power of the steam engine soon pulled us up when needed.

We stopped at our friend's house on the outskirts of Leeds to have a thorough check over all the bearings and moving parts. Wesley was over the moon. His eyes were popping out of his head as his mam produced plates of stew for all of us. Wesley's father was home this time and he was delighted to catch up with us again.

On the road again and we reckoned we might get home without more water but we planned a short stop outside Wetherby for another check up so we threw the suction hose in the beck where we had refuelled previously. Next stop was the Great North Road or A1 as it is known now through Wetherby then about 1hour home. We pulled into our farmyard absolutely worn out with James needing an emergency stop in the Royal Oak, which was conveniently situated alongside our farm house.

A good cleanup before parking in the other corner of the yard did not take long because the tractor was still rusty and dirty after years of neglect. The next phase was to buff up all the metal skin and working parts before a decent paint job.

"James was ecstatic as I was too before he made a stern announcement in which he said loudly for all to hear "This tractor will look magnificent when we get it all painted up and put into showman's livery Brian but I'm telling you now that it will not leave this yard until it is finished, no matter how long it takes us."

"Ok James" I replied I'll remind you of that when you get itchy feet at the start of next season." James gave me a large grin before disappearing back into the Royal Oak.

Having the tractor nearby made more work much easier. One major problem still to fix was the generator. The original had been, somehow, removed probably for scrap or for another engine. It amazed us that it had been removed without anyone noticing because it was huge and would have needed a crane to get it down. It was a few months before we found a generator in a scrap yard and it turned out to be in good order. We put new bearings and carbon brushes in before re-installing it in front of the smoke stack.

During the next few months work on our engine continued at a pace. All the rust was removed section by section then the cleaned area was sealed with special paint to preserve it. The twisted bass tubes were refitted to the canopy supports. We checked all the wiring for the canopy lights and special low voltage DC globes had to be obtained and fitted. Eventually the tractor was ready for a proper paint, but where was the painter. Prospector was so large that we needed a painter to come to her rather than us taking her to a painter. As summer was approaching and better weather forecast it looked likely that a spray painter could tackle the job. A local man was asked to come in and talk to us about preparation needed to ensure a good finish. Certain parts would need to be removed to allow the painter to operate smoothly and he insisted we had to spend many more hours smoothing the undercoat ready for a series of finishing coats to achieve a superfine finish to his liking.

A few days before we were due to remove certain parts and rub down the under coat James rushed over to our yard full of excitement like a kid a Xmas.

As usual I was busy collecting eggs when he finally caught up with me and gasped out, "Oh there you are Brian I spend half my time searching for you. Have you seen this latest edition of "THE WORLDS FAIR" yet?" James was waving a newspaper in the air for me to see.

"How could I James," I replied "You Know I only get to see it when you've finished reading it. What's so exciting in it anyway that's upsetting you so much?"

"Its next weekend Brian. We nearly forgot about it. We'll have to get cracking. It's time for the big engine rally at Chester-le-Street in Durham. We 'aven't much time. I'll need to get some good steaming coal from somewhere and pack all our gear ready for the road."

"Hang on James, slow down, it's too late already. It will take us two full weekends to get there unless you can get a low loader to shift us in time." I pronounced.

James answer to all this was "Nah young man thou, doesn't understand. We'll take t'big un. She's fast enough to get us there on Saturday ready for the rally next Sunday so long as you can get the weekend off that is. I'll go and see Charley {my Dad} when he gets home. It'll be alright you wait and see.'

"Whoa! Whoa! There James, you've forgotten one important thing. You've always said that Prospector will never leave our yard until she's finished and she still has to be painted."

"Aye that's right trust you to put a spoke in t'wheel." James came back at me. "Well you see I've been thinking about that and I realised that it would be a tragedy if we went to all the work and cost of putting on the finishing coats only to find there was something mechanically wrong then we would have to start again. Better we find out now. A 60 mile trip each way to Chester-le-Street would sort out any problems prior to painting Her then we would know."

"Alright with me James if Dad agrees. I could light the fire on Friday night after school and bank it down ready for an early start on Saturday morning if that's what you want.

"Right you are then young man that's all settled, I'll look out for Charley coming home and leave the rest up to you." Was James final remark as he strode away.

I was already in bed when Dad arrived home that evening so I never made contact with him but next morning as I was brewing up a cuppa mam came in and said, "James Alderton called in last night after you went to bed. He talked to dad, something about a road trip to Chester-le-Street. Your Dad said as long as you caught up with your work and homework you could go although it means more work for me but I'll get by. You'd better be ready for a busy time on Monday morning before you catch the bus to school."

"Gee thanks mam, I will help out as much as I can before I go and on Monday morning, because I start with woodwork, it won't matter if I miss the early bus and have to catch the next one. Mr Metcalf is a darling really and won't punish me anyway."

Chapter 6

CHESTER-LE- STREET RALLY

I found it very hard to believe that we were actually going to Chester-Le-Street and taking Prospector. I realised that we had no chance of winning any prizes but just to be there. Oh! Wow! This was going to be the busiest few days of my life. I had to prepare the tractor and my personal needs, with very little help because James had to catch up with his plumbing work. Everything around home had to be up to scratch, hens, ducks, geese, pigs, garden, firewood for Mam and school work. Hey who cares I was going to the rally!!!

After tea on Friday evening I set a small fire in the firebox of Prospector. As I sat on the footplate watching the flames licking away at the kindling I was uneasy. Was this trip actually going to happen? Would Dad suddenly burst into the yard and stop me from going? Would James be held up with some urgent plumbing work? I had not even set eyes on James since he first mentioned the rally. Pat told me that he was working day and night to get on top of his work. Never the less I continued to build up the fire until I could start putting some coal on as well. Boy! Oh! boy was I tired. I balanced the old kettle on the fire shovel as we usually did to make a cup of cocoa then I felt some-one put out a hand to steady mine on the shovel as a quiet voice whispered in my ear, "You'd better drink some of that cocoa now and get yourself to bed Else'wise you will miss the boat in the morning."

James had just arrived home and I had dropped off to sleep holding the now boiling kettle still balanced on the shovel. We shared a hot drink and I left James to finish off and bank down the fire for the night. I went inside to clean myself up and crawl into bed. I was awake before dawn had fully broken switched off the alarm before it woke everybody else up and once dressed headed down to check the fire taking half a loaf of bread and some butter with me. I freshened up the fire topped it up with more coal and boiled the kettle for tea and toast. The steam pressure was just enough to start the engine to pump more water into the boiler. I was toasting lots of bread on the coal shovel when James joined me for a quick breakfast before setting off after a final check of the works and boiler. Knowing his parents always rose early in the bakery we called in to stock our larder for a couple of days on the road. James told me that Pat would catch us up later in the van after settling the Kids down with her Mam. He said the kids were pretty disappointed not to be coming but the Austin van could not fit us all in for the return journey and in fact we were badly crammed in as it was. Time was not in our favour due to each of us having serious commitments on Monday morning. The tractor had kerosene running lights but they were next to useless on the highways. We had no choice but to find somewhere to park up until the following weekend and all return in the Austin van.

I reminded James of the farm near the show ground where we camped up last year.

I said, "Maybe the farmer will let us camp there overnight on this Saturday before the rally then leave the tractor for the week like we did last year. He seemed very happy with us then so let's see if it works again this year."

James's reply was "Aye well that might be ok and it will save a lot of messing about on Sunday morning. We should be able to get a good start to the ground and find a good spot to park up before the rush starts. You know what it's like all the exhibits turn up at once and then pandemonium sets in with tempers flaring as the organisers try to please everyone at once."

It was early Saturday morning when we left our yard and steamed down the village to collect a box full of food from the bakery. Everything was running smoothly so off we went. The road to the A1 was (and still is) very narrow and winding so we had to travel slowly, however being so very high up made it much easier to see any oncoming traffic but we had the road, about two miles to Minskip, all to our selves. About 1 mile further on I turned left onto the A1 amongst a number of lorries and cars. The other drivers must have been amazed to see this great big tractor heading into and through Boroughbridge at about 12 miles per hour.

The Great North Road or A1 as it is now known was only 3 miles from home then it went all the way to Chester-Le –Street and beyond all the way to Edinburg. Once travelling on the A1 except for water stops we had no problems. Due to previous trips along this highway we knew where we could pick up water conveniently but because of the extra bunker tanks we would only need a few stops. There was a good clean beck near Boroughbridge where I topped up all the tanks whilst James oiled and checked all the moving parts, and there are plenty of those.

Back in those days there were very few split lanes or dual carriageway so the other traffic had to work hard to overtake us. Fortunately the road was quite flat and straight for most of our journey so we kept up a good speed. There were only a few villages along he way and Darlington was the first major town. James elected to run in second gear until we cleared most of the town then into top gear all the way to Durham city. We stopped at a familiar watering spot just outside town for a nice lunch of Mrs. Alderton's bread and pies. I Filled the bunkers with enough water to get us to our destination James had the oil can and checked the bearings but all was well.

Chester-Le-Street was now only as short run

and I used my lollipop signal to turn right off the A1 just before the town. The side road was actually a main road that, according to the signpost led to Hartlepool and Sunderland. I had made the lollipop during the week to stick out of the cab so we could let other drivers know where we were turning off. Pride of the Road was open with no cab so drivers could see our hand signals but on Prospector we were hidden in the cabin to a greater extent. I utilised an old tennis racquet with an extended handle then cover the mesh with some bright red fabric which seemed to work well. If we wanted to stop or go straight we waved the signal madly straight upwards. Going right was the worst so I waved it out of the side over the great big wheel. No one ever ran into us so it must have been effective.

There was a short sharp hill running away from the A1 and the farm gate was just a little way and close to the hilltop. The gate was open so we were able to just steam straight in. The farmer, Mr. Phillips came hurrying out of the barn to see what was going on. He was amazed to see the monster tractor parked in his yard. When we climbed down off the footplate he recognised us immediately and welcome us back. After Mr Phillips got over the shock of seeing us he commented, "So there you are we were wondering if you would be coming again this year as you promised, but when we didn't get a letter we thought you mustn't be coming this year but here you are. Have you sold the other tractor or just swapped it for this one?"

I left James to explain our actions and organise a berth for the tractor whilst I settled the fire and wiped up most of the oil and soot from her works.

Mrs. Phillips insisted that there was plenty of bath water and then we were expected to dinner, bed and breakfast once we had cleaned up. As I have said before, the hospitality of the people, especially farmers that we met on our travels never ceased to amaze us. Driving either of the tractors took a good deal of concentration as well as hard physical work and we were always ready for a good bit of spoiling wherever and whenever we arrived.

After a good long soaking bath, change of clothes I went down to the farmhouse kitchen where, judging by the smell a hearty meal was being prepared. Once The Phillips family had completed their day's work and we had eaten a fantastic meal, we washed the dishes then settled down to a good old natter about our recent exploits. Both of our hosts were absolutely amazed to hear about our year's events and the outcome. We were really disappointed about the condition of Prospector but promised that next year would be better.

I was out of bed and dressed just as dawn was breaking but when I entered the farm kitchen it was obvious that Mrs Phillips was already about and preparing breakfast. I excused myself to attend to the fire and boiler but all was well. It only needed the clinker removed, the fire opened up and more coal added.

After a hearty breakfast we bade our hosts farewell so as to get on the road early. We expected to be one of the first tractors on the field but a good many were already there cooking breakfast on their shovels in true engineman fashion. It appeared that the early birds had pulled in the afternoon before and were ready for the fray.

James gave them a big blast on the whistle as we entered the gate and of course most of them replied with great gusto. We were wondering where to park when a small group of officials approached. "What the hells going on here, "James asked" "We don't usually get a reception committee at the rallies."

One important looking chap approached the tractor and greeted us with, "Thank Goodness, at last we have a big fairground engine. We have a fun day lined up for you lads if you are up to it. See over yonder up on the rise we have a White Brothers Gavioli fairground organ from Durham. It's the biggest they ever made with 149 keys and needs some driving. How do you feel about joining them and see if you can make it sing for us. It means that you will miss all the other events of course but it should be compensation in itself. What do you say to that."

James looked at me then asked, "Well young man what do you reckon then?"

"I think it will be a great honour for us and I am happy to give it a go if you are"

"Aye well that suits me then so lets see if we are up to it."

We travelled up to the organ which was nearly as big as our rig. It comprised of a four-wheeled trailer with a turntable under the front. It was like a huge pantechnicon lorry. The whole of the side panel lifted up and was propped up on legs to support it and reveal the works.

There were monkeys playing the drums, ballerinas gyrating in formation, bears dancing in the centre. My! oh My! what a dazzling display all lit up with coloured globes. There were masses of gold leaf on the figurines and lettering and even before we fired it up it was a great display. We were told that a doctor from Durham city had rebuilt and renovated the organ at great expense and he was waiting to hear the music. The whole lot of the machinery and music was enervated by the use of punctured cardboard panels hinged together in a long chain. The panels were about 3ft long with holes punched through them to activate the keys. There were quite a stack of panels each with a different song selection.

The owner of the organ was on hand to hook our generator to the organ then show us how to run it. Once the electric cables were connected we were given the instruction to fire the engine. Thank goodness I didn't need to steer anything as James carefully opened up the power valve and set it all in motion. The volume of the music was massive and we were told later that the local kids were dancing to it a mile away. The owner of the organ had made a wonderful job of setting it up and it needed very little tuning and other adjustments on our part. The biggest jobs were firing the engine and changing over the punched cards as they ran out.

Supplies of water and coal were delivered to us by tractor and trailer as time went on, then a catering van arrived to feed us workers. Lots of hot tea was not a problem as we had the kettle hanging off the firebox as usual.

James and I were having a great old time when Pat arrived to join in the fun. Early in the afternoon the organisers came for a chat with us. They pointed down the showground to where another huge fairground engine was approaching. He said quite apologetically. "I 've Arranged for the Rover to come up and relieve you chaps. You 've had a dull, old morning up here on the hill so we organised a fun spectacle to cheer you up but you'll need all the steam that you can squeeze out of this old girl."

Dull morning! He had to be kidding. We were having a great old time making music and entertaining every one on the show ground.

Never-the-less we unhooked after the end of the next panel and moved away for Rover to move into place. Rover was a burrell locomotive of a similar ilk to Prospector but a little smaller. Her owner had spared no expense on Rover and she was magnificent. The paint work and livery would have put a rolls Royce car to shame. There was heaps of gold leaf on the lettering and the whole thing gleamed in the sun. The driver just walked around her with a fluffy yellow duster wiping off the odd oil spot and any dust. All the brass work, and there was plenty of that, gleamed like gold. We were humbled to say the least. Even Prospector herself seemed to hang her head in shame, however we had work to do.

"Now you lads listen up. We have been challenged to a tug of war by the local fordson tractor dealer. He has welded up a tandem framework of steel so that he can run two tractors side by side then a further two in front of those. He has 4 of the latest fordsons to fit into the frame. As you probably know each one is 56 horse power and will need all you can pull out of your tractor to beat them so: what do you reckon are you lads up to it. Imagine the shame if they beat you"

James lifted his old cap and scratched his head saying, "Well if my fireman is up to it I reckon we just might be able to tackle the job." Turning my way he asked, "Well pal, what do you say then."

I answered, "We've never tried a big pull on rubber covered tyres but with wheels this big we should be able to get enough grip to beat them because they are on rubber tyres and all. Our weight should be a help too, even if we don't try to pull them along the traction we get should even out the rubber on grass."

Driving the organ had left us a bit low on steam so I poured a heap of coal into the firebox as we drove down the field and carefully reversed into line to get a good straight pull. Most steam tractors only drive on one rear wheel due to the fitting of two large steel driving pins through the wheel hub and through the axle flange of the drivers side wheel. Because these machines do not have a differential gearing in the back axle like most other vehicles they have to leave out the pins in the other side. When a bit of extra grunt is needed we have to jump off and fit the pins in other side as well. This creates a problem because the tractor will only travel in a straight line when both sides are pinned. Because we needed lots of traction we put all the pins in place then we were ready. The boiler pressure was slowly creeping up as we took up the slack cable. The starter man called out "Are you ready then." And James told him to start the tractors off. He opened the steam valve so that the fordsons were able to drag us slowly back towards the red flags. The organisers had used a very long steel cable retrieved from a local coal mine. It was deigned to give us a really long haul to improve the spectacle. James carefully adjusted the steam valve to make the fordsons think they were winning. They were spinning their wheels and digging big holes in the grass but they were winning. We were very close to getting beaten when a very old engine man tried to gain access to the driving platform.

He shouted angrily in my ear. "Get out of my way I'll bloody well show you lads how to drive this thing. You can beat them tractors easily if you know what the hell your doing."

James tapped the old man on his head with the fire shovel telling him, "Get to hell out of it you daft old bugger you'll get yourself killed." He was standing right up against the huge driving wheel so James had to get ready to stop in a hurry. The old bloke decided discretion was the better part of valour and climbed down out of the way.

All this had distracted James from his main purpose but he still had time. James looked over the back of the coal bunker then he shouted "Only a few yards to go pal. Are you ready when I count three?"

"Yes pall, lets do it I called."

"Right you are then, One, Two, three, go."

As James opened the steam valve I pull out the double high pressure lever thus filling the second cylinder with fresh high pressure steam instead of the used steam from the first cylinder. Because the low pressure cylinder is twice the size of the high pressure one we more than trebled the power. Only then did I look out in front of the tractor and realised that many of the spectators had crowded round us to watch this mighty spectacle end. I grabbed the chain of the steam whistle just as the boiler reached full pressure and blew the safety valve. I hung onto the whistle chain as spectators grabbed kids and ran for cover. With the front wheels off the ground we set off up the field at full speed. Nothing would stop us now. We pulled the fordson tractors with all eight wheels spinning madly, past the red flags to the winning position but James did not stop there we kept on going until we reached the hedge at the far end of the field. As we stopped, triumphantly, with Prospector huffing and puffing happily I climbed down from the foot plate to stretch my legs and get some fresh air when I was almost knocked flat. The old geezer who had threatened me before had run all the way up the field after us.

He wrapped his arms around me and gave me a great bear hug. He had streams of tears pouring down his face as he declared. "By heck young man I've niver seen nowt like that afore. I'd have 'ooked onto them lads before they knew what hit em and dragged them away round yon field. Not you lads you let them buggers think that they had beaten you, then you 'it 'em hard. Well done you two."

Many years later with modern safety regulations in place everywhere I wondered what would have happened if that old mine cable had broken in mid tow or some one had failed to get clear of the tractors as we raced for the hedge.

The tractor was sitting there against the hedge. I had to remove the pins from the nearside wheel so that we could reverse away from the hedge and head off homewards. Because our mad chase had landed us on the top side of the grounds we decided to cruise around to where Rover was still powering the organ. We especially wanted to have a good look over her paint job with a view to getting some ideas of our own for Prospector. We neither of us ever expected that she would ever come up to the same specs as Rover, (there wasn't enough money in our camp) but we could always try. The owner driver said, "Don't worry lads, Rover had looked as bad if not worse than Prospector when we started,"

We stared, fascinated watching Rover at work with the organ until we realised that it was time we put Prospector to bed for the week. We drove back to the farmyard and dropped the fire before settling her down for the weeks rest. Mr and Mrs Phillips were waiting for us with a huge farmhouse meal on the table. They both congratulated us on our day, we did not realise that they had spent most of the day at the rally and watched us demolish the fordson tractors. They invited us to return next year and stay with them. We promised to return with a nice coat of paint on the old girl as well. After hugs all round we climbed into the Austin van with Pat at the controls. Pat said something to me about parking in our yard to unload before I realised that I had slept all the way home. I walked into the house to see my mother relaxing in the lounge in front of the television.

I said to her, "My mam you look comfy. How much do we have to do in the morning?

Mam grinned at me and replied, "Aye lad there's nowt to do in t'morning. It's all done see. Apart from you usual feed up of course.

"How ever did you manage to get all the eggs packed as well as all the feeding? Don't tell me our Jean actually helped you then."

"Naw of course not. You know our Jean better than that, lad. Your school pal Trevor turned up after lunch on Saturday afternoon. He was a bit disappointed that you weren't here but he insisted that he would stay and help me. I gave him his tea when we finished the eggs and he fell asleep on the lounge so I threw a blanket over him and left him there until this morning. Trevor helped out all day today then I gave him some eggs and veges for his Mam before he went home on the bus about 5 o'clock. We had a good weekend. He's a right grand lad is Trevor but he was really sorry you were away."

"Well it's great to know I have real friends like Trevor. His Mam and Dad are the same and his sister Hillary is lovely too."

"Aye well we managed ok but how did your weekend go" Mam asked. "I wasn't expecting you back for a while yet."

I explained that we had left the tractor at Chester-le-street until next weekend.

Mam snapped at me, "I hope you don't expect to go next weekend your Dad will have plenty to say if you do."

"Naw, it will be just a straight forward drive and Pat can manage that now she has had a bit of a go."

Little did I know that this would be my final trip with James and any of his engines. I was in my final year at high school with GCE exams at the end. I did extra well in my exams as expected then applied for a special traineeship at Perkins Diesel factory at Peterborough which was 150 miles away and boarding with a family in Crowland in nearby Lincolnshire.

Postscript

CHANTELLE

I have decided to write a post script to Shake Rattle and Roll which takes place much later in my life after emigrating to Western Austalia.

My granddaughter is called Chantelle and it will eventually take a few years and a whole new book to tell you all about her but, of course that's another unfinished scenario, although it's a very important part of my life with plenty of deliriously happy days and a fair amount of pain and sadness. However this story has very little to do with my granddaughter and is the story of a steam tractor and the reason for the title will become clear with time.

After moving to Harvey when I was in my early 50's I became involved with a restoration enterprise at the historic workshops in the small south-west town of Yarloop. The workshops had been, for many years, the nerve centre of a large timber getting outfit scattered throughout the south west of our state of WA. In the early 1900s the developing world had a great thirst for timber, especially hard wood timber suitable for railway sleepers. The worlds railways were expanding rapidly with the introduction of steam driven locomotives. There was no better timber for this purpose than the eucalyptus trees of Australia, and Western Australian Jarrah and white gum were among the best available, and there were large quantities ready to be harvested.

Millars Timber and Trading moved into the south west forests and began to extract timber mainly in the form of railway sleepers and most of these were exported around the developing world on sailing ships initially then moving on to steamships as they became more acceptable.

As Millars moved away from the city to harvest more trees they had to build their own infrastructure to get their equipment out into the forests and recover the timber back to the ports.

One of the problems was that most of the best timber was growing in the forests covering the Darling Scarp, a ridge of fairly high hills of over 1000 feet in height running fairly close to the coast and parallel to it from North of Perth, right down to Busselton. The hills rose very steeply from the coastal plain and were tough going especially in the days of heavy horse and bullock teams.

Once the government railway system was established along the flat coastal strip south of Perth and became available for public use, Millars interconnected with it. They built a system of narrow gauge railways suitable to negotiate the steep climbs over the ridge. Once over the ridge they set up many small steam powered mills to cut the timber into manageable sizes to facilitate transport to the harbours. These mills used up the waste timber and saw dust to feed the boilers of the steam engines. We talk about recycling today but those guys were masters of it very little ever went to waste. Face cuts were often used for fencing and garden sheds. I have, even today seen pigs housed in face cuts and sheep yards made of them.

The company had to build a large base and repair workshops at Yarloop. They set up foundries and machining shops so that they could be independent of the manufacturers in England because it often took about 6 months to a year to get the parts over by sailing ships.

I don't intend to go into the history of the workshops and timber industry because that's another story but I will mention the sudden closure of the workshops due to a devastating cyclone called Alby, which severely damaged the aging buildings that housed them in the late 1970's.

A very dear friend of ours, Collin Pusey, had collected many steam engines and pumps from around the state and set them up for public display in a shed at the now partly renovated workshops. I worked with Collin and a dedicated band of volunteer steam fanatics to rebuild and run these huge steam engines. The largest twin cylinder engine was 380hp with a twelve foot diameter flywheel. The steam house is open and running on a number of Sundays throughout the year and we attempt to teach the general public about steam power and its great significance to the timber industry and other power needs of industry in general.

One day, Collin was approached and asked to provide a home for a half sized replica steam tractor, which was in very poor condition having been neglected for many years. Collin, knowing of my involvement with real, full sized steam tractors in England offered the tractor to me to undertake it's restoration and hopefully it's operation at Yarloop and elsewhere in the future. Without hesitation I jumped at the chance and set to work re-engineering some of it's features. Then stripping, cleaning, and repainting the rest. I designed and built a steam whistle for it and obtained a couple of passenger trailers to tow behind it and give the kids a ride. The restoration was a great success and gave me and the visiting kids many days of pleasure. I modified a 6 x4 car trailer so I could transport the little tractor around the state to various shows and fetes.

At last we get to the story of Chantelle. I decided to call the little tractor Chantelle because it reminded me of my granddaughter of the same name. Like the little girl, the tractor needed constant supervision once the fire was lit and like the little girl she was always dirty. Due to the wood fire generating heaps of smoke and soot that poured out of her and the fact that it had, like it's real ancestors, a total loss oiling system. This meant that all the oil that it needed to run and lubricate the moving parts ended up liberally spread over her and the driver, in spite of which I loved her dearly, The girl and tractor alike, I found both impossible to keep clean and no sooner had I finished one end than the other end would need my attention again. I believe it's called "LOVE"

One memorable Sunday afternoon I was wiping the oil off the tractor, which was standing close to the steam house doorway whilst waiting for more kids to fill the trailers when a tall, thickset gentleman walked over to have a good look at the engine. He stood in front of the tractor and called out to someone behind him.

He called out "Look, Look, come here love. Here's 'Thomas'. Come and see."

A little girl who was probable close to three years old walked around him and into view. She smiled at me with a look of intense anticipation because, apparently she was an ardent fan of 'Thomas the tank Engine' then as she turned to look at the tractor her face slipped off and turned to great scorn and utter disgust. She stood akimbo with her feet widely spread apart, then put her little hands firmly on her waist with elbows outstretched and looked upwards into the face of this giant of a man who was apparently her dad and spat out with much vehemence;

"Don't you know?" (huge breath) "That's not Thomas." (huge breath) "Thomas is a train." (huge breath) "Thomas goes on the rails."

Another huge scornful breath, then "That's Terrence" (huge breath) "Terence is a tractor". (huge breath) "Terence goes on the road".

With that pronouncement she stumped off in disgust and went into the steam house. She was so disgusted that she steadfastly refused a ride in the trailer. Her dad appealed to me for support but I was only able to agree with his daughter whilst doing my best not to laugh in his face.

Afterwards I said to Collin after recounting the incident,

"Poor little girl, fancy going through the rest of her life with a dad as thick as that". We travelled to many towns with Chantelle and a favourite was a long way out in the eastern wheatbelt at Kukerin where the local committee catered for visiting show people. They allowed us to set up camp in the bushes around the local footy ground so we could stay all weekend. We took our tent and set up a barbecue around a fire place dug into the ground with a circle of stones. There was always a rodeo on Saturday evenings and mud racing for cars in an artificial creek along the rear of the grounds. In spite of the remoteness of the town there was always a massive display of machinery much of which we played with. We dug large holes and filled them in again. We dug up a large area of dirt and levelled it off again with the vintage machinery just to show how clever we were and how well the machines carried out their various tasks. One good feature of the show that was that, unlike most of the similar shows around our state, they did not cater to the horsey crowd who normally dominated country shows, apart from the rodeo crowd there were no horse activities at all.

On the Sunday morning we almost blew Chantelle and half the show ground into oblivion. I lit the fire and stoked it up to start the day the travelled across to the side of the oval to start entertaining the crowd and giving free rides to all the kids, around the perimeter of the oval. The fire was stoked up to the maximum and the safety valve was blowing off steam when I suddenly realised that, although the boiler pump was going, the boiler was not filling up.

I had maximum heat going into the boiler, which was now getting very low on water. I had to take immediate action to kill the fire or get the pump working before the boiler blew up. It was at that moment that I realised that the boiler designer had made a couple of serious, critical errors in design and construction of the boiler in spite of strict regulations. The firebox did not have closure flaps on the ash pan to shut off or even control the air supply to the fire and I remembered that when working in the firebox during restoration there did not appear to be a fusible plug in the dome. It is necessary to drill a hole right through a special threaded plug and pour molten lead into it to seal the hole off.

In the event of the boiler overheating for whatever reason the lead melts out of the plug and allows a stream of water to flow onto the fire and extinguish it quickly.

I was really starting to panic when I thought of a possible solution. I could not leave the tractor for safety reasons and I was desperately trying to move the spectators and general public away from the area. I called out to my wife Sandra asking her to run back to our camp site and collect the metal lid from our camp kettle. Whilst Sandra was away I put the tractor out of gear and started the engine. The exhaust steam vented into the smoke stack which tended to increase the fire so I opened both cylinder drain taps to remove as much steam as possible until Sandra returned with the kettle lid. Once she handed me the lid I placed it on top of the smoke stack with a heavy spanner on it to hold it. The kettle lid carried out a number of functions so long as it stayed in place. Firstly it smothered the fire with smoke and exhaust steam from the engine then all the exhaust steam had to exit the same way as the smoke, that is, through the fire bars and into the ash pan thus preventing fresh air from entering. The fire quickly went out or so it appeared at the time.

Whilst the engine was running I realised that a non-return valve on the side of the boiler that admitted water to the boiler and prevented steam blowing out was not rattling like it normally did so I hoped that was the reason for the pump failure. As soon as the steam pressure dropped to zero I carefully remove the inspection plug and removed the return spring which was in good order. Below the spring there was a steel ball bearing but I couldn't see how I could get hold of it to clean it and the seat below, and of course it was boiling hot That's when I remembered that the electronic anti-theft device on my utility was actuated with a small round magnet attached to my key ring. The magnet was just small enough to fit into the plug hole and lift the ball out so I could clean it. I found that a small piece of scum from the bunker tank had slipped through the filter screen and held the ball off it's seat.

It took only a few minutes to re-assemble the valve and start the fire again. There was now a sizable crowd around me, and the tractor and a queue of kids lining up for rides. All I had to do now was relight the fire and wait until I had enough steam pressure to travel. I lifted off the kettle lid then opened the firebox door to put some kindling in and relight the fire. Imagine my surprise and delight to see a mass of red-hot coals in the box just waiting for some air to make it blaze which did almost instantly. The boiler still contained enough boiling water to get enough steam to run the engine and pump. The water was still at boiling point and quickly began to make steam. It only took a few minutes to get the pump going again and with fingers and toes crossed for luck I started the motor. The valve rattled away contentedly for the rest of the day. No harm done except for my nerves and a couple of serious lessons learnt. I had a large piece of brass casting at home which I put in my lathe and made a heavy, neat shiny cap to fit the smoke stack. This we carried with us at all times in the event of future emergencies. The rest of the day went off without a hitch and we returned to our tent for a feed and a good night's sleep to fortify me for the long drive home the next day.

Over the coming years we attended the opening of a railway museum and a large commercial airfield. We visited a number of town celebrations and sporting events. We attended every agricultural show within range and a boy scouts jamboree in Perth It was only when I found out that I had a serious health problem needing urgent surgery that I arranged for the owner of the Dardanup Heritage park near the town of Dardanup to purchase Chantelle. The last I heard she was living in comparative peace in a large shed at the park.

www.ingramcontent.com/pod-product-compliance
Lightning Source LLC
Chambersburg PA
CBHW071913290426
44110CB00013B/1367